EXTREME SONNETS

EXTREME SONNETS

CONTEMPORARY POETS

Edited by Beth Houston

Rhizome Press ℞ Bradenton, FL

Publisher's Cataloging-in-Publication data

Names: Houston, Beth, editor.
Title: Extreme sonnets , contemporary poets / edited by Beth Houston.
Description: Bradenton, FL: Rhizome Press, an imprint of Beth
Houston Publishing, 2020.
Identifiers: ISBN: 978-0-9988196-3-1 (pbk.)
Subjects: LCSH Poetry. | Poetry--Collections--21st century. | Poetry,
Modern--21st century. | Sonnets. | BISAC POETRY / General
Classification: LCC PN6101 .E995 2020 | DDC 821.92--dc23

In memory of Bob Evans
August 11, 1936-July 2, 2019
a fine poet
an engaging friend
a scholar and tender of trees

In addition to providing a wealth of accurately metered and well-rhymed poems, Beth Houston's anthology demonstrates the astonishing range of subjects and tones that the sonnet can accommodate when excellent writers turn their hands to it. Included in these pages are studies of nature, science, politics, love, religion, and family that are by turns bittersweet, funny, heart-wrenching, mordant, and ironic. Equally arresting and enjoyable is the structural variety of the poems. Many scrupulously and effectively observe the stop signs that mark off the sonnet's traditional divisions. Others sweep over the boundaries between octaves and sestets, stride across quatrains, or employ a closing couplet less as a summarizing feature than as an extension of a narrative or argument initiated earlier in the poem. Whether read straight through, or dipped in and out of, this book offers wonderfully entertaining fare both for sonnet aficionados and for the general reader.

—Timothy Steele

When Giacomo da Lentini came up with the sonnet during the thirteenth century, he must have been pleased with a form that seemed perfect for his favorite theme: love. He may have foreseen how future poets would play with the sonnet's fourteen lines by altering the rhyme scheme, the structure of the form, and the placement of white space. The examples in this impressive collection, which intends to present the form in easily recognizable "classic" ways, would probably not have shocked him, as every example in it is true, or not far from true, to the first Italian models, those that eventually morphed from them to the ever-familiar Petrarchan and English sonnets, and then out to the dozens of variants still being produced today.

What I suspect da Lentini could not have foreseen is the inexhaustible range of uses to which his "love poems" would be adapted, and with what boundless success. When I began reading the manuscript, I kept track of the changes to the form. But soon I stopped noting those and began to marvel at the near-absence of the love theme once thought to be the sonnet's natural purpose, and became aware, instead, of how much else this gathering of gifted and skillful sonneteers were conveying with a sturdy form clearly capable of accommodating every theme, subject, tone, and effect.

Here, in a very selective list that could have been much longer, are some of the things these poets are packing into my favorite fixed form that has kept me reading with uninterrupted feeling, pleasure, surprise and enduring engagement:

Jerome Betts scolds Shakespeare; Leslie Monsour passes judgment on Creation; Bruce Bennett confesses to a crime; Wendy Sloan discovers an enduring incorporation of mourned and mourner; Jean Kreiling sings, of course; Midge Goldberg creates characters who create an imaginary town; Claudia Gary slyly asks more than a favor of the reader; David Stephenson speaks for an honest dog; Kyle Potvin votes for sin; Lisa Barnett comments on the male nude; Kevin Durkin pays a warm tribute to my former profession; Duncan Gillies MacLaurin records a parental betrayal; David Gwilym Anthony has an encounter that goes sour; Chris O'Carroll keeps repeating himself; A. M. Juster prays; Jane Blanchard is forced to let go; Debra Wierenga makes up for time wasted on early obedience; Gail White speaks for Penelope—sort of; Eric Meub spits out a harsh, painful story; Alexander Pepple begs for a sign, and Joseph Salemi provides a magisterial close.

Thank you, poets, for a book to be treasured; thank you, Beth Houston, for putting it together; thank you, Rhizome Press, for taking on its publication at this difficult time. And—oh yes, I almost forgot—*grazie mille*, Giacomo, for this tough, elegant little box of words that will hold just about anything!

Rhina P. Espaillat

Why make the effort to write a sonnet? Quite simply: the joy of it. Why else create something that takes darn hard work when it has no pragmatic purpose (besides wooing, or course)? When readers enjoy and appreciate the sonnet, that's icing with a juicy cherry on top.

As editor at Rhizome Press, it's my privilege to facilitate for both writers and readers the pleasures of formal poetry, starting with this collection of sonnets, my personal favorite form.

Those of us who enjoy formal poetry likely have our English teachers and literature professors to thank for that. Most people with a high school education could pick the sonnet, ballad, limerick, villanelle, and a famous excerpt from Shakespeare on a multiple-choice final. A month or two later they would likely just be able to identify each (including the excerpt) as "a poem" along with any free verse poem.

It's not news that the relevance of formalism dwindled once *vers libre* grabbed hold of poets' collars. By the mid twentieth century a good handful of prominent poets had gone so far as to brand formalism regressive, and even fascist. But the skepticism of all things "old" that dominated in the "new" era of world wars, atomic bombs, and fascist dictators didn't deter all poets. Many indulged in formalism, albeit cautiously, and often temporarily. Some boldly wrote predominantly formal poetry, and a few created literary journals dedicated to it.

As I see it, the two crucial qualities those formalists handed us are distinctive, well-wrought, fine-tuned forms and the musicality inherent in those forms, fixed form or nonce. A form's precision compels the poet's laser scrutiny of every line, every word, every syllable, as well as meaning, sound, and the whole's unity and effect. Ironically, the tighter form's strictures necessitate freedom to explore new possibilities the poet wouldn't have otherwise considered.

Imagery is the heart and soul of all good poetry, both formal and free verse. (Heart in both senses, physical and emotional.) Imagery resonates when it is unique and precise and has something to say, even if simply *look*; look at *this*. But musically, the formal poem—the form itself—delivers a more complexly structured, a more elegant, composition: it is, quite simply, in and of itself more musical. And for the astute poet, the structure inspires even more refined musicality.

Once formal verse comingled with free verse, fresh content infused traditional forms, and experiments rendered new renditions of the forms themselves. Poets now feel free to play with various poetic elements, and even elements incorporated from other arts. And at least some free versers are casting a fresh glance at formalism.

The looser formal poetry widely written and published these days is what I call *semi-formal*: a fusion of strict formalism and free verse. Meter, rhyme, and/or tight "fixed" structure is alive and kicking mainly thanks to journals that feature every brand of formalist poetry.

Able Muse is perhaps the most influential bastion of formal poetry today. Originally billed as "a review of metrical poetry" that included formal poetry, interviews with formalist poets, essays about poets and poetry, a featured poet and artist, and "the first e-book of formal poetry on the web" (per the *Able Muse* geek editor) when the online journal first appeared in 1999, the Able Muse enterprise has since assembled an impressive portfolio that includes print versions of its online journal, online and print anthologies, including one devoted to translations, a respected press of print books and ebooks, annual contests with prestigious judges, and Eratosphere, an array of administered poetry forums and workshops for its 8,000-plus registered members. Though its offerings now include free verse and fiction, *Able Muse* still caters to various iterations of formal poetry. For his twenty-plus years of persistence in that area, founder and editor-in-chief Alex Pepple deserves a medal.

At Rhizome Press my goal is to expand by contracting—to provide a vehicle just for *extreme* formalism that is characterized by regularity that restricts exception. Ideally, extreme poetry sticks to impeccably consistent structure; pure rhyme (allowing for regional variation) that adheres to a clearly defined repetition scheme, with rhymes close enough together that they register; meter that is constant, with exceptions only for stresses, and then rarely and only when the context calls for it, but with no added or subtracted syllables (though allowing for elision, and colloquial and regional pronounciation); and when a line is broken, the parts taken together equal a line with the requisite beats and rhyme.

I use the terms *extreme* and *semi-formal* for the sake of clarity; they are not meant as value judgments. Of course, each of us is entitled to a personal preference.

In this first anthology, I've allowed more exceptions to *extreme* meter and rhyme than I'd originally intended. Those exceptions make sense poetically, and the sonnets that take liberties add to the "read's" overall quality. And all the poems are quite close to perfect form.

Is there really such a thing as perfect form, not to mention a perfect sonnet? Well, is there really a perfect snowflake? Who isn't struck by the delicate lacework of a snowflake's perfect symmetry, by a perfect crystal that is "just" ice. Yes, perfect, even though each nucleates—comes into being—around a particle of dust. That clear ice appears white due to each crystal flake's tiny crystal facets' (crystals within crystals) diffuse reflection of the whole spectrum of light. And though each snowflake is a perfect hexagon, and no two snowflakes are alike, each has enough similarities to certain others that it fits into one (or more) of several distinct categories. Just for starters.

(Pardon the analogy: I'm a poet; it snowballed.)

The intricate balance of defined structure and dazzling variation inspires appreciation, if not awe, in those of us who really *look*. And true appreciation is an experience of pleasure.

Writers of perfect sonnets, like the poets you'll find here, are of the ilk of those who really look. Readers who look *through* them/*with* them will find much to enjoy.

CONTENTS

I

II

V

I

WATER BEARER

Each dawn, before the sun devoured the shade
and seared the arid land, a potter strode
down to the well along a dusty road
to fill a well-used water jar he'd made.
As he returned one day a stranger said,
"Your jar is fractured. Anyone can see
you waste your time and labour fruitlessly.
The water spills along the track you tread."

The potter answered, "Though it leaks it still
retains enough for me, and I would not,
for all its flaws, discard my battered pot.
It has a further purpose to fulfill."

Where he had passed, a radiant display
of flowers bobbed to greet the breaking day.

~ David Gwilym Anthony

MAKING IT

A smoke-white sky and darkened pines beyond
the window glass. A bright red journal on
the desk—nine pages scribbled, nothing spawned
that I will claim as mine. Crows peck the lawn.
I notice all my clothes are black: the shirt,
the socks, the pants. I fight a metaphor.
We've lost. *We're* lost. It's not exactly hurt
we feel. Creation helps us bear much more
than this. Change follows change: just breathe to meet
the next. I'm reading William Stafford. *What*
the river says is wisdom's thin disguise.
Appeal to something shadowy. Too neat?
I don't think so. The poem that helps, clicks shut
and opens up. Why make it, otherwise?

~ *Thomas Zimmerman*

IMAGINING DAVID READING *THE FIELD*
for Rhina P. Espaillat

I think how David would have loved your book.
The formal poems all perfect, clear, precise.
Each sonnet an exemplar. Each device
Mastered and marshaled. He knew what it took
To get all right like this: a lifetime spent
In humble strict devotion to one's craft;
Not one thing left to chance; draft after draft
Until that final phrase comes. What it meant
To put that first, yet know that's not enough
Since one must live and be what one can be
And love what one must love. Yes, he would see.
You somehow pulled this off. Tender *and* tough,
Like him. He would have reveled in the ways
This gave him boundless joy and earned his praise.

~ Bruce Bennett

To the Poet Who Thinks I Praise Promiscuously

You're right, I like to compliment my friends,
And I have sometimes been one who pretends
To like things when I don't. Haven't we all?
My mother taught two lessons I recall:
Politeness breeds persuasibility;
Say nothing if it risks hostility
Or pain. But now you call it cowardice
And insincerity, a soulless kiss
Intended to dismiss a date and close
The door, a phony smile, a languid pose.
Dear friend, I'm honest, but I have a heart.
It feels all wrong to criticize the art
Of those I prize. Blind caring reassures.
Or does it reek of childhood? Mine, or yours?

~ Leslie Monsour

Shakespearean Sonnet

Perhaps a typo in some dog-eared book;
scant onionskin that saves a cherished hand;
the fragile glamour in the smell and look
of wildflowers; earnest orators' unplanned
assertions; strange locution in a rushed,
ambivalent, inexpert turn of phrase
voiced in a midnight Ouija question, hushed,
reheard verbatim on ensuing days;
anonymous graffiti: there's no squelching
such subtle art, and when we chance to hear
some boor who's cheered us hitherto by belching
break out as an impromptu balladeer,
and find no supple beauty in his song
that feeling may be genuinely wrong.

~ *Max Gutmann*

18

AT THE SUMMER POETRY FESTIVAL

after Dick Davis's "At the Poetry Reception"

Ah there she is, all siren-like and fair,
Looking for blurbs, no doubt. I like her hair.
As for the manuscript she's bandying,
I've heard it's so-so, but I'll praise the thing.
My Pulitzer and sultry, southern lilt
Routinely do the trick—she'll all but wilt
Into my arms. I see she wears a ring.
So much the easier to have a fling.

She's caught my gaze. I'll raise my glass and wink.
What luck, she has my book and wants a drink,
I'll meet her at the bar. *What have we here?*
Sign it for you? With pleasure, yes, my dear.
No pen? No matter. Later on we'll go
And look for one inside my bungalow.

~ Leslie Monsour

The Poet, Trying to Surprise God

The poet, trying to surprise his God,
composed new forms from secret harmonies,
tore from his fiery vision galaxies
of unrelated shapes, both even & odd.
But God just smiled, and gave His know-all nod
saying, "There's no surprising One who sees
the acorn, root, and branch of centuries;
I swallow all things up, like Aaron's rod.
So hold this thought beneath your poet-bonnet:
no matter how free-seeming flows your sample
God is by definition the unsurprised."
"Then I'll return," the poet sighed, "to sonnets
of which this is a rather pale example."
"Is that right?" said God. "I hadn't realized . . ."

~ *Peter Meinke*

Unrepentant Sonneteer

Why should I stifle what I hear inside,
my blood and brain both urging me to rhyme
in sonnet patterns, while arranging time
in iambs, five per line? The critics chide,
preferring poetry unbound by beat,
unfettered by the old fourteen-line frame,
and unrefined by rhyme. But none would blame
the other arts for standing on sure feet:
Picasso dared, but still used shape and line,
Stravinsky's modern sounds required old notes,
no dance or architecture simply floats—
the ground must anchor every new design.
What arrogance should move me to discard
a form that drew both Updike and the Bard?

~ *Jean L. Kreiling*

SLUSH PILE

In some respects I like this, even though
the workmanship's not great. Who'd rhyme 'today'
with 'day'? This one's arcane: what does it *say*?
Two down now; just two hundred more to go.
Call that a poem? It's prose! And this one's so
Poetic. Why must people disobey
the basic rules of syntax? No. No way,
and No, and No, and No, and No, and No,

and . . . Oh. Here's something special: see it shine.
It coruscates: a lamp of burnished gold
revealing vistas heretofore unseen.
I sense the presence of a noble soul
who dares to go where none before has been . . .
Ah, I recall it now: it's one of mine!

~ David Gwilym Anthony

8 A.M. LITERATURE CLASS

I've stayed up all night marking their exams.
They've done well, with the usual exception.
I'm weary, and exhaustion's hammer slams
Me into half-sleep. I have no conception
How I can lecture on the *Tales* of Chaucer.
I set a pot of coffee up for perking
And when it's brewed, I spill it, and the saucer
Holds a brown puddle. Man, this isn't working . . .
Maybe some Benzedrine will clear the mist
But that won't kick in for another hour.
I have to teach right now. I know the gist
Of what I plan to cover, but a sour
Taste in my mouth is pushing me to say
Class cancelled . . . take your tests and go away.

~ *Joseph S. Salemi*

TOUGH PROFESSOR SONNET

Crazy! He flunked the lazy wafflers right
and left while all his colleagues let them slide
on by like sheep through dip. At any rate
both high- and single-handedly he slowed
their march toward mediocrity, that root
rot of our time (he said), where we've mislaid
the standards that we used to know by rote:
Democracy's a sloppy-minded slut.
Of course they hated him. They squealed like pigs
beneath the knife when he returned a paper
bright with blood. But because they were square pugs
who paid tuition they paid the piper
too and he was fired. In time the pegs
grew fat in their round holes. He died a pauper.

~ Peter Meinke

On My Blindness

When I consider how my light is spent
—Milton, "On His Blindness"

When I consider how my eyes are spent
Just grading essays for an adjunct's dime,
My talent sapped correcting grammar crime
For those who don't care, much less document . . .
Darn fragments, run-ons, shifts. It's complement,
Not compliment! And commas—you'd think I'm
The devil one kid called me. Life's primetime
With dangling modifiers—*that's* torment.
Just when I think prose can't get any worse,
Some plagiarize, and I'm called back to waste,
Soul-crushing work that's stolen, and I curse
The work sublime I never wrote, with haste
I turn in grades, I dash this formal verse
So after liver, ice-cream I might taste.

~ Beth Houston

A Sonnet of Complaint

Great shade of Shakespeare,
                    I—B. Montague—
Was no mere progress-sweller, all agree,
But, even so, did not receive my due—
A role confined to Acts One, Two and Three!

Once brought to life upon the playhouse boards
Why do I disappear and leave the stage,
Forsaking fair Verona's words and swords,
Your smash-hit tragedy's unwritten page?

I might have made a difference in Act Four
And then, the star-crossed lovers not alive,
Have played my ever-helpful part once more
With fitting farewell lines to end Act Five.

Despite your fame and monumental Folio,
I am, *Signor*, the chance you missed!
                         —Benvolio.

~ Jerome Betts

THE MOVIE SCREEN

is mirror just as well as window: dreams
scream *cinema*, our shadows on a wall,
and so I speak the names. There's *Annie Hall,*
King Kong, and *Dr. Strangelove.* Lives, it seems,
enhanced and captured in a frame. *The Bride*
of Frankenstein, Pulp Fiction, Vertigo,
A Streetcar Named Desire. We think we know
there's more outside the box, but can't decide
how wild we want our minds. *Some Like It Hot,*
The Maltese Falcon, Throne of Blood, High Noon,
The Silence of the Lambs. The types so soon
imprinted on the psyche, deep as thought.
The Searchers, Cabaret, The Seventh Seal.
Shaped fantasies have made our lives more real.

~ Thomas Zimmerman

WET DAY IN THE READING ROOM

The dribbly twins, the woman with a tic
Who drones about the blacks, the bubbling chest,
The vacant-eyed, the squashed, the dull, the sick,
Are here for shelter and a heated nest.
Hunched up below a line of local views
And one large print, *The Fighting Temeraire,*
They simulate attention to the news.
The smell of mouldy raincoats fills the air.
Stone letters are still proud, high over all
The condensation and its crooked ways
Down scribbles that vermiculate the wall,
The spreads from which the glossy models gaze
And notices forbidding smoke or spit—
Magna Est Veritas . . . Praevalebit.

~ *Jerome Betts*

ON ESPERANCE BAY

So pebble-rich a beach will never miss
A mere fourteen shaped oval, heart and pear.
See here, a reddish, orange-brown one. There,
A semi-oval, semi-kite. Then this:
A yin-yang dancing on a heart of gold.
But now it's gloaming time; it's hard to see
Their glamour anymore. And only three
Of these fourteen will have their fortunes told.
I somehow doubt these sleeping beauties mind.
What's it to them this Scottish sonneteer's
Account's soon twenty-two in terms of years
Spent sheltered on this shore? They're deaf and blind
To rise and rush and fall, to this kiss blown
Across the sea, to being left alone.

~ Duncan Gillies MacLaurin

SONNET FOR POE

So all the nuts are loosening, the bolts
bemoaning matter's fate. When will the damned
old mansion clatter to the ground? Like colts
that romp the paddock bare, like hacks who jammed
their penny-words in clauses stale for hire,
your frayed-wire thoughts spit sparks but won't turn off.
Your propositions chomp through time, on fire
like Keats in bed with bloody midnight cough,
a brood mom bitten by her litter, king
gone fishing dreaming that his wound will heal.
Remember when you gave that girl a ring,
the stone as blue as sea, as moods surreal,
as blood before a feeling-giving cut?
Your mind has locked a door that doesn't shut.

~ Thomas Zimmerman

SONNET ON THE DEATH OF THE MAN WHO INVENTED PLASTIC ROSES

The man who invented the plastic rose
is dead. Behold his mark:
Undying flawless blossoms never close
but guard his grave unbending through the dark.
He understood neither beauty nor flowers
which catch our hearts in nets as soft as sky
and bind us with a thread of fragile hours:
flowers are beautiful because they die.

Beauty without the perishable pulse
is dry and sterile, an abandoned stage
with false forests. But the final results
support this man's invention: he knew his age:
a vision of our tearless time discloses
artificial men sniffing plastic roses

~ Peter Meinke

DUNDERHEAD

You have no earthly means of challenging
Oblivion. Its menace snags your fears;
Its malice smothers love; its madness sneers
At composition. Every note you sing
Might just as well, well, never have been sung.
You think by fastening your windows tight
You'll cheat that hound from hell? Hell, every night
It stands outside and drools with triple tongue!
So much for noble dreams. So much for rules.
So much for truth and beauty. In the end
You'll go out howling. How can you pretend
Compliance is a safety net for fools,
Yet practice it yourself? You dunderhead!
What good is recognition once you're dead?

~ *Duncan Gillies MacLaurin*

AT THE MUSEUM OF THE BOOK

Now folks, the first exhibit is a book,
the docent droned, that only we can touch
with latex gloves. So be content to look.

(Librarians had no one left to hush;
now this museum occupies their space.
The stacks are closed, and research pretty much.)

We think that size and format once were based
on folds in hand-laid sheets, producing leaves.
These letters, inked with type, would fill each face.

(Though others left us lessons to retrieve,
who'd bother reading shelves of printed texts?
So, here they're safe from all us oafs and thieves.)

Please move along; these glassed-in artifacts
are cordoned off. The printing press is next.

~ *Ted Charnley*

II

On Learning the Harvest Moon Is an Optical Illusion

That giant orange vision in the sky?
Don't trust it. Screw the songs and poetry,
it doesn't shrink while rising low to high—
of course not. But the moon I think I see?
That splendor should be caused by something real,
some angle of refraction, atmosphere.
But no, no reason, nothing to reveal—
it's only in my mind these sights appear.

I'm mad. Enough so that I want to turn
away from awe, depend not on my mind
but fact alone, that cold, hard rock. Unlearn
this beauty that relies on being blind.
But something in me craves this lunacy—
 It's beautiful. And big. It has to be.

~ *Midge Goldberg*

BIG BANG

That time of year thou mayst in me behold
— Shakespeare, Sonnet 73

All space-time's years you may in me behold.
Here, nature's dust gets tricky as the show
Rolls on, my body's elements as old
As God's Creation. How old? I don't know.
Some guess ten billion years. And then there's life,
Four billion just for cells, for DNA,
Their molecules and atoms, bliss times strife.
All mixed in some real crazy complex way.
But orchestrated. Light's fleshed-out ballet
Embodies movement, costumes, scenery,
Chic music topped with bows, spring's huge bouquet,
Blue curtains pulled by hid machinery.
    Hey death! —Love child of space and time, I snatch
    Their dance to hatch this verse for you. From scratch.

~ *Beth Houston*

Starlight, Star Bright

When I gaze at the sky on a clear night
I know that all those twinkling points of light
Are dime-a-dozen suns like ours, a sea
Of other worlds extending out of sight.

I pick one out and think how it might be,
A giant gas ball burning blindingly
As unimagined planets float nearby,
Each one a snowflake of geology,

A thought of God. Observed from its strange sky
Our modest sun would hardly catch the eye
Of anyone there picking her own star
To ponder, wish upon, or reckon by,

To conjure in brief visions from afar,
To notice out of all the stars there are.

~ David Stephenson

LUNAR ECLIPSE

Our neighbors gather in their heavy coats.
The youngest ones are thrilled to stay awake.
With towels as capes, they race the passing boats,
not noticing the chill beside the lake.
And then the change begins—the children rush
to huddle up. They watch the full blood moon,
red across its face, spreading like a blush,
as if it caused the darkness coming soon.
The loons sense otherworldly things; they wail
like mothers warning toddlers near the street.
A small girl plays. Her shovel fills a pail.
She builds a village at her mother's feet.
The earth aligns. She yawns as toes dig deep
into the sand. Secure, she falls asleep.

~ Kyle Potvin

THE SUNSET WATCHERS

They stand along the concrete fence that wends
between the bluff's green edge and gritty path,
their faces reddened while the sun descends
by cool degrees into the bay's curved bath.
The younger couples murmur, point, or kiss.
The older pairs stand side by side, hold hands.
Joggers slow down, and tourists reminisce
about their morning rambles on the sands.

The palm trees, leaning toward emerging stars,
clatter more keenly as the breezes shift,
while far below, six lanes of homebound cars
rush like the surf. The moon begins to lift
above the city, her reflected light
shining on all who face the coming night.

~ Kevin Durkin

Meteor Shower

A comet strews its path with cosmic crumbs,
Motes, castoff scraps of solar system stuff,
Specks inconsiderable, yet enough
To coruscate. Around our planet comes,
A yearly, fire-eyed impresario
Bent on refashioning each humble grain
Into a drop of incandescent rain,
The star of its own brief but brilliant show.
We snag bits of debris in high, thin air
And frenzy them to glow and disappear.
Some drill our night sky, lunge with white-hot spears,
Others trace threads as fine as baby hair.
Alike to dainty wisp and lancing thrust
We *Ahhh!*— dust amply entertained by dust.

~ *Chris O'Carroll*

HOROSCOPE

The stars are using dice and bird entrails
To come up with a short-term plan for you;
You will receive updates on the details
Via upcoming bolts out of the blue.

In the meantime, both you and your free will
Should just continue on your dreamboat course,
Since you will still have several weeks to kill
While life, the snake you're charming, gathers force

To implement some fresh impediment
And let the subtle aftermath unfold.
But what will follow that experiment,
Your next adventure, cannot be foretold,

Because the stars themselves don't even know;
They're making all of this up as they go.

~ David Stephenson

To a Catalpa

Most of the year, you look like a buffoon,
Your pods awkwardly long, your outsize leaves
Like oafish hands that gangle from their sleeves.
So when, for one unlikely week in June,
Your air froths festive and your earth is strewn
With blossoms frilled around a color scheme
Of sun-gilt tear tracks, twin streaks gold-on-cream,
Amid fine veins and spatters of maroon,
And fragrance syrup-rich though light as dew,
You startle us with hope we, too, might be
Capable of that moment, or those few,
In which quotidian absurdity
Contrives somehow to conjure or renew
An efflorescence of divinity.

~ *Chris O'Carroll*

The Face of Things

The eye knows leaf from hummingbird at once,
Even at distance, even dusk; discerns
Among the flecks of green an immanence
Of sudden flight, as though the will returns

A subtle wavelength, visible as light.
The green of foliage, the leafy green
Of matching feather, then a clever sleight
Of surface that conveys a deeper scene,

The heartbeat underneath. The eye both *in*
And *measuring* the world—an inborn task
That even camouflage won't contravene
Cannot help pointing back behind the mask.

Depth cannot hide. And so it flutters, sings,
Betrays itself upon the face of things.

~ *D.R. Goodman*

HARMONICS

My teacher showed me how to touch the string
as lightly as a miller moth that floats
as much as lands, and pull the bow to coax
the overtone, the note's thin ghost to wing
into the air above my violin.
These secret sounds sleep up and down the length
of every string, but only sing beneath
a finger perched precisely as a pin
on a map to mark where you haven't been.
The way telescopes find more stars between
the ones the eyes can see. Or dogs collect
tall tales of scents our noses can't detect.
Or poets pluck the mind's gut core to play
unspeakable music the soul would say.

~ *Debra Wierenga*

Lyrics from a Distance

It makes you cry out loud, her violin;
the notes without a voice, the keening strings.
They almost rise and soar, she almost sings
to you among the crowd, then reels it in.

You want her closer now, to hear your words
accompany her music, if you can.
But when the encore ends, you're just a fan
who wants to meet her backstage afterwards.

And there, with all your knocking on her door,
you'll stand before her, tense, and try to read,
your starstruck words a stutter, nothing more.

Her face will blur, her knowing smile recede;
then, from afar, your lyrics rise and soar.
It isn't what you want, it's what you need.

~ *Ted Charnley*

WHALE WATCH

Late on a summer day, down at the pier,
The whale watch boat anchors across from me.
The tourists disembark, but I can't hear
If they saw any whales while out at sea.
I search for signs in faces passing by:
What will I see, if I just stand and wait,
Some wondrous look, a light within an eye?
I want to stop someone and ask him straight,
"Just tell me, did you see a whale or not?"
But I can't bring myself to ask. To go
So far to catch a glimpse of what they sought,
To fathom whale—some telltale sign must show.
Today I say no other prayer so well:
That they did see a whale, and I can tell.

~ *Midge Goldberg*

LINES IN BAKED CLAY

Between the trees, the soil dries out and splits,
Smelling of apples perfumed by the sun;
In warm bruised fruit the wasps fret browning pits.
Over the orchard hedge, the furrows run
Down towards the ghost that troubles ranks of maize
Whose tassels dip, rise, dip, to mark the stone
Parching their growth, town pavements, drains and ways.
Now, where they cross, an oak-tree stands alone.
A plane still quarters, as the light turns gold,
To read the landscape's labyrinth of lines
And flesh out tales the scraps of Samian told,
Post-holes and sockets touched by plunging tines
And coins' dumb faces that the ploughman found
Where the winged shadow ripples without sound.

~ *Jerome Betts*

GHOST ORCHID

Dendrophylax lindenii

Through sawgrass swamp, roused gators stir up muck.
Domed islands rise. Dense hardwood hammocks root.
    Live oak, mahogany, bald cypress suck
Up nutrients. Thick vines through thickets shoot

Past banyan, gumbo limbo, poisonwood.
Vast stands of slash pine shadow fern and palm
    Awash in brute green gnarl-kneed arborhood . . .
Sweet, fruity dusk scent saturates the calm

Surrounding pop ash near pond-apple trees—
One wisp white flower floats on humid air
    Uplifted by midsummer heat, brief tease
Angelic, thin stem stitched through bark somewhere . . .

    Night listens . . .
                One lone sphinx moth that by chance
Evolved to taste her nectar hears her dance.

~ Beth Houston

48

WEB

After "Design" by Robert Frost

A black and yellow garden spider toils
In counter-clockwise interstitial coils
To join the cartwheel radii of its snare
Then occupies the hub and hangs midair.

What forces have inspired it to resemble
A flower blossoming whose petals tremble
In noon's light breezes, fooling butterflies?
The lie turns into truth before my eyes.

But let's be fair. The spider's masquerade
Must not be misconstrued as wrong or bad;
Nor should the trussed, convulsing copperwing
Be seen as innocent or suffering.
Darwin explains it better than The Fall:
Nature selects. It's hard to watch, that's all.

~ *Leslie Monsour*

NO HELP

The chipmunk, bright-eyed, mouth still filled with seed,
dangled from the cat's mouth. She let it go,
purring, and though I knew there was no need,
I held it for a moment, just to know
for sure that it was gone. There was no breath,
though someone might have sworn it was alive,
pretending slyly, counterfeiting death,
the way the small and meek act to survive.
No help for it. That mouthful was its last,
crouched in the grass, or hunching by its hole,
the sunlight bright, perhaps a shadow cast
by cloud, its little life not in control
of anything, yet seeming safe and free
as anyone could hope or wish to be.

~ *Bruce Bennett*

KEEPING THE CAT IN

It goes against her nature. Yes, I know.
But when she's in, she can't do any harm.
I let her out again, and watch her go
straight to the spot where I expressed alarm
and snatched her up, then watched the baby mouse
hop off and make its slow way through the grass.
The only place for her is in the house,
but that's not fair to *her*. I'll let it pass
again, relent, then find her with fresh kill.
And so it all repeats. There's no way out.
But meantime there's my coward's way. I will
feed her. *Perhaps she will forget about
the world outside,* I think. I buy some time,
so I won't feel so bad about our crime.

~ *Bruce Bennett*

THE HOARDER

My children think I have too many cats.
I don't agree, but I know what it means:
They think I'm getting senile, breeding bats
In this old belfry. Children don't know beans.
Wait till they're old and see their crepey skin
Like washed unironed taffeta, their veins
A railway map of Europe, while they spin
Unheard-of nightmares in diminished brains.
Before your body is a nuisance more
Than a delight, before you'd welcome death
Sooner than one more catheter, before
June weather chills you with December's breath
And your unlovely skin needs warmer furs,
My dears, you'll love what sits on you and purrs.

~ *Gail White*

MOOSE

The puppy had big feet, just like a moose.
He stood on spindly legs, ears at a tilt—
one up, one down—thick black curls hanging loose.
He was an Airedale mix, solidly built.

The Berkeley life was perfect for the dog.
He met his friends around, outside cafes
and shops, and feats too bold to catalogue
were laid to him. Those sea-blown, foggy days

he followed her most everywhere she'd go.
Except New York. For that they'd have to wait
for her to settle, or a tumor grow.
She sent for him. By then it was too late.

What more to say? He suffered and he died,
and every time she thought of him she cried.

~ Wendy Sloan

SNAKEBITE

He was an Easterner, and didn't know
In Texas there's real danger on the ground.
Nobody warned him. Guess they never thought
It necessary to explain. And so
He went out poking through an Indian mound
Maybe for shards or arrowheads. He caught
A glimpse of something curious at the lip
Of one small crevice, reached in like a fool—
The rattler struck him squarely on the palm.
At first he thought it nothing but the nip
Of insects. He ignored it, kept his cool,
Went home without a shadow of alarm.

Three hours later, to his consternation,
The doctor prepped his hand for amputation.

~ *Joseph S. Salemi*

OVER THE EDGE

The wind was strong and at our back all day
So we sped merrily across a sea
Awash with floating patches of debris:
Old crates and sea chests bobbing in the spray,
Rot-splintered planks and oars and the odd stray
Overturned lifeboat drifting randomly,
All striking our hull lackadaisically
And spinning, sinking on the ricochet.

The boats they sent to stop us have turned back
And there are no birds trailing in our wake;
We sail beyond the maps and charts alone.
And now the waters swirl and skies grow black
And in the distance vast waves rise and break
And we are doomed. If only we had known.

~ *David Stephenson*

HANDS FOLDED TO CONSTRUCT A CHURCH AND STEEPLE

Hands folded to construct a church and steeple,
A roof of knuckles, outer walls of skin,
The thumbs as doors, the fingers bent within
To be revealed, wriggling, as "all the people,"
All eight of them, enmeshed, caught by surprise,
Turned upward blushing in the sudden light,
The nails like welders' masks, the fit so tight
Among them you can hear their half-choked cries
To be released, to be pried from this mess
They're soldered into somehow—they don't know.
But stuck now they are willing to confess,
If that will ease your grip and let them go,
Confess the terror they cannot withstand
Is being locked inside another hand.

~ *Mark Jarman*

IN THE ALTO SECTION

Beethoven's Ninth Symphony

You sit behind the orchestra, spellbound
by complex chemistry you've heard before:
a measured mix of breath and time and sound
decreed by small black icons in the score.
You recognize these runes, for you've been trained
to translate this arcane calligraphy—
to be a catalyst for unexplained
excursions into immortality.
At last you stand; at last you get to sing,
your mortal, mid-range voice admitting you
to this inspired amalgam. Finally
your notes are needed for the rendering
of gold: believe, and count, and on your cue,
supply the center of the alchemy.

~ *Jean L. Kreiling*

Seasonal Song

What warm and spiny hope, what tiny glow
now kindles like a phosphorescent cell,
pale bioluminescence on a swell
of steely inner sea? Faint as a low
blue flame, it settles in, and left to grow
unchecked would spread its bloom across the tide,
bright streak of optimism just beside
the monstrous ocean's darkest ebb and flow.
Winter has struck the flint of this strange light,
has tricked the mind, and now the season's turn
means change is possible, and all that's fine
and clear may yet infuse a future bright
beyond all reason, 'freeze' revised to 'burn'
as easily as water, once, to wine.

~ D.R. Goodman

HYMN

Picked warm right from the tree, one perfect peach,
When sliced atop vanilla ice cream, screams
I love you louder than tired, bitter themes
Of fire and brimstone. I hear sweetness preach
On nature's bounty, let her sugars teach
My cells to thrive, like each fresh sunbeam streams
Through juicy peach flesh, so now my flesh gleams.
Each luscious bite inspires a sacred speech
On miracles; what prudes impeach, I praise:
As I taste peach and cream, we three commune!
I reach, and stone-cold spring tree's blossoms blaze
With light converting fruit. I lick my spoon,
Rejoice I'm saved by grace aimed to amaze
As peach and I French kiss, and blissful, swoon.

~ Beth Houston

Winged Presence

The damselfly, at rest, folds up her wings
as if in prayer. She waits, perfectly still,
observing what the present moment brings.
Then silently, she holds her pose until
her instinct guides her to move on. She glides
with ease above the grass, the hills, the streams.
She has no need to stop and analyze
her path, or be concerned with hopes and dreams.
Before she is herself, the damselfly
must molt a dozen times; then she'll arise,
she's finished with the struggle. She can fly
unburdened by illusion and disguise.
Her jewel-like body takes up little space;
her existence is a silent hymn to grace.

~ *Diane Elayne Dees*

AMAZING TO BELIEVE

Amazing to believe that nothingness
Surrounds us with delight and lets us be,
And that the meekness of nonentity,
Despite the friction of the world of sense,
Despite the leveling of violence,
Is all that matters. All the energy
We force into the matchhead and the city
Explodes inside a loving emptiness.

Not Dante's rings, not the Zen zero's mouth,
Out of which comes and into which light goes,
This God recedes from every metaphor,
Turns the hardest data into untruth,
And fills all blanks with blankness. This love shows
Itself in absence, which the stars adore.

~ *Mark Jarman*

THE ROAD TAKEN

Youth's urgency permitted no delay
and many paths diverged. I didn't know
which one to take or where I ought to go,
and settled for a broad and trodden way
because it offered light and company;
but as my friends dispersed along the road
I travelled on alone and often strode
in haste through where I had no wish to be.

At evening everything becomes opaque,
and circumstance has turned the track I chose
back on itself, much nearer now to those
remembered byways I shall never take.
This is a light to me when dark is near:
the paths diverged but all at last led here.

~ *David Gwilym Anthony*

Paper Town

The fictional town of Agloe, New York, was invented as a copyright trap by cartographers to help track infringement.

The tourists driving through look at the map,
the empty road, the map. They clean their glasses.
Not knowing anything about this trap,
the nearby townsfolk shrug, when asked. Time passes.

Soon myths arise about the mill that closed,
the families that were forced to move away.
All sorts of dire causes are supposed.
Day trips are planned, with cheese and Cabernet,

to find anything left behind, to scout
for chimneys, cellar holes, a single door.
Since it's a shame to let a town die out
like that, someone decides to build a store,

painted in weathered tones of creams and grays,
hoping to recall the halcyon days.

~ Midge Goldberg

One-Way Ticket

Cwm Cynfal and the Ceunant: the valley
and gorge of the River Cynfal

They closed the line and just the track remains.
The miners' railway where we used to play
in far-off summers, when I came to stay,
echoes with the ghosts of long-gone trains.
Cwm Cynfal and the Ceunant ring with wild
unchanging songs of childhood: years away
mean nothing here. When I returned today
they called to me, and knew me as their child.
The rest is altered irretrievably.
My kin died years ago or else moved on:
no point in staying once the work was gone.
How few there are who still remember me.
Those broken ties will not be whole again.
The line is closed and just the tracks remain.

~ *David Gwilym Anthony*

ROADSIDE CROSSES

This is a state where nothing marks the spot
Officially. They crop up now and then
Out on the freeway, or in rustic plots
Sometimes, near S-curves in the country, when
The corn's knee-high: a cross, or even two
Or three, made out of poles or boards, white-
Washed or painted. They seem to have a view
Of nothing at all: only the blurred lights
Of oncoming cars, and the eighteen-wheelers
Roaring by. Memory has a harsh sting—
Blown back like the fine grit that settles
While you walk here now— no special healer,
Merely a friend or brother stopped to bring
A can of flowers, to place among the nettles.

~ *Jared Carter*

Shades of Venice

For all its beauty, Venice has been cursed.
The shades of Shylock and von Aschenbach
Still lurk behind closed doors. Soon after dark
Sebastian Flyte inspires a giant thirst
On balconies above the Grand Canal,
Where discontented sons of millionaires
Console each other, high on Baudelaire's
Philosophy of life, *Les Fleurs du mal*.
Come Carnival they'll all be sporting masks,
Assuming alter egos by the score.
They'll personate Poseidon as before
But now feel free to flaunt their pocket flasks.
A lethal dose elicits no surprise.
Each gondolier is Charon in disguise.

~ Duncan Gillies MacLaurin

HOTEL BALCONY

This crib is bolted firmly to the wall.
From here I watch the sea, its shades of green,
And save the junebugs crashing on the screen
From dying upside down. With stupored crawl,
And plodding flight, they make fine toys, as psalms
Break loose from sparrows passing by. I glance
At people milling home and think of ants,
Then nod at someone leaning on his palms
Across from me. He stares at something lost
The way we gaze from windows of a train
At places we won't ever see again;
And life unwinds, as if it had been tossed
Like a Surprise Ball from our place of birth,
Unwrapping trinket glimpses of the earth.

~ *Leslie Monsour*

LOS ANGELES IN FOG

The morning fog obscures the corporate towers,
shrouds the shorn palms, slips through the glaucous boughs
of eucalyptus, dampening the hours
when call girls sleep and dealers start to rouse.
Pacific in its provenance, it covers
unsheltered youths, cops on their crooked beat,
the cardboard beds of uncommitted lovers
too crazed and poor for anyone to treat.

When will the sun burn through this fog, expose
syringes floating on advancing seas,
the strung-out billboard starlets in repose,
the citrus flames of oil refineries?
When will we view the wide Cahuenga Pass,
its freeway shoulders glittering with glass?

~ *Kevin Durkin*

On the Death by Drowning of My Favorite New Orleans Restaurant

The corner of Canal and Carrollton
sheltered Mandina's, where for seventeen
years every Saturday they poured me one
black Russian followed by trout amandine

or the best shrimp loaf on the whole Gulf coast.
But now the watermark is at my eyes,
the floors have rotted, and the stolid ghost
of a decayed refrigerator lies

prone on the sidewalk. And I'm shedding tears
over a stack of dishes, one of which
I'll steal in memory of those seventeen years
that made their gumbo and my life so rich.

Come back, my love! Serve me on shining dishes
my weekly miracle of loaves and fishes.

~ *Gail White*

WHEN YOU FIND ME STARING AT THE OCEAN

Because you ask me what I'm looking for,
I tell you *nothing*—but that's not quite true.
I stare in this direction to restore
my sense of indirection; to see through
a sea of obligations, plans, and jobs;
to float instead of swim; to leave behind
the getting and the spending amid mobs
all headed in their own directions, blind
to all but their to-do lists, dutiful
and destined to dry out into cliché.
I've done that. Right now I'm responsible
for little more than breathing in the spray
from waves I watch. I know that if I stare,
I might find everything or nothing there.

~ *Jean L. Kreiling*

SIGHTSEERS

A string of pelicans in gliding file
Traversed the setting sun. We watched awhile
Before the captain shared an observation:
"The pelicans die early, from starvation.
They waste ashore, unable to take flight;
They haven't lost their wings, they've lost their sight.
The reason they go blind is said to be
The force with which they plunge into the sea
To nab their catch; it massacres their eyes."

Hard nature made them rash instead of wise.
They threaded to a point. We watched them drift
Above horizon's gaudy hues and sift
Through sun's last glimmer sipping darkened tide,
Where night awaited, opulently eyed.

~ *Leslie Monsour*

NAVIGATOR

I raised the anchor; sails flashed out unfurled,
then filled; I set a course, h t t p://—
and started out across a cyber sea
in search of fellow feeling in the world.
I wandered where the winter seas were pearled
with scattered islands of affinity,
whose harbours sometimes felt like home to me,
calm havens when distress and discord swirled.

Seafarers slightly known and swiftly gone,
some here to listen, some with things to say:
those strangers warming in the light that shone
from empathy had little time to stay.
Minds met a moment, touched and travelled on
to look for something lost and far away.

~ *David Gwilym Anthony*

CROP DUSTER

There's nothing quite like flying your own plane,
Even a little single-engine one.
When you're aloft, beneath the blowtorch sun,
Above the sprawling corn and bean domain,
Your every humdrum worry slips your brain.
I always hate it when a job is done,
When I've found the right field and made my run
And must descend and walk the Earth again.

I usually deliver pesticide.
I've killed my share of bugs. But I'm for rent
For fertilizer, too, for that same fee.
Depending on who's paying for the ride
I rain down either death or nourishment,
Like any god, but without mystery.

~ *David Stephenson*

BRYCE CANYON

Nature's long, patient vandalism spree—
Ice that claws crevices, the thaw and flow
That shreds red rock, dissolving a plateau—
Shapes this fantasia of geology,
This landscape of frail sculpture or debris:
Arches that frame the view and are the view,
Precarious high boulders perched askew
On shafts of knobby instability.
Elements tussle and collaborate
In the off-kilter grandeur of this place,
Joined in a flux that fashions and erodes
With gestures that demolish to create,
As, in the vaster canyons of deep space,
New worlds gestate each time a star explodes.

~ *Chris O'Carroll*

EILEAN MUNDE

Graveyard Island, a burial ground for several
Scottish clans, located in Loch Leven

The Highland mist conceals a sacred isle
Where green of moss embraces gray of stone
That marks the grave of one who fell to guile
Of clansmen who betrayed him to the throne.

In life he donned the mantle of a laird
And rested hand on hilt of sword or dirk
But slept unarmed by winter hearth he shared
With those who broke his bread and shamed the kirk.

The daughters of the dead succumbed to snow
And prayed with frozen lips for shelter's grace.
At death's approach they glimpsed a jeweled bow
That bridged the clouds from loch to holy place.

But duty tethered falcons to the wrist,
And souls foreswore the sunrise for the mist.

~ Elizabeth Spencer Spragins

BLOODLINES

They're pictured wearing baubles carved from bone,
woad-daubed and fur-clad, flaunting tribal scars.
Such incorrect, such crude depiction mars
the memories embedded in the stone
and in my blood, my every chromosome.
Why paint their culture worthless next to ours,
those folk who traced the movement of the stars
and built Stonehenge before the birth of Rome?

Their mysteries live on within each cairn
and megalith, though little else remains:
like us they learned what pride and progress cost.
If we could call their spirits to return,
would they stand silent, awed by all our gains
or stricken, seeing everything we've lost?

~ *David Gwilym Anthony*

THE WEIGHT

The unforgiven hang around my heart
like a charm bracelet fashioned out of lead.
They weigh me down—the living and the dead—
and though I often will them to depart,
they always find their way back. Father, mother,
the husband who embodied sins of both,
surround me with their brutal weight of truth
about myself. And there are also others
I think that I've forgiven, and yet still,
I feel them pressing hard against my soul.
This isn't something that I can control
through sheer intention or desire or will.
What will it take to tear apart this chain,
to melt the weight, obliterate the pain?

~ *Diane Elayne Dees*

CHARM BRACELET

She separates each tangled charm with care:
A skate, a girl clad in a choir robe,
A four-leaf clover, praying hands, a globe—
Souvenir of the '64 World's Fair.
It was her husband's job to clasp these links.
She loved how when he worked, he never spoke,
Leaned close—his clumsiness an inside joke,
His playful way to hold her near, she thinks.
Why did she rush to pull their hands apart?
These simple gestures are the greatest loss.
Another try: She drapes the chain across
Her wrist and braces it against her heart.
No use. There is no way to join the ends.
Without his help, the bracelet dangles loose.

~ *Kyle Potvin*

To the Hillslope

My friend and I traversed the hillslope, where
The boulders share their angle of repose
With mountain foliage as it steeply grows.
We sat upon a rocky outcrop there.
My friend and I let breezes toss our hair,
And we tossed careless words between us. Those
Uncaring words soon made us feel like foes.
How fast our humors soured, our tempers flared!

We never went again to that same place,
Although without our presence it appeared
To be the most serene of all domains.
Perhaps our roots weren't ready for the space
That slants through rough terrain, so multi-tiered.
Instead—for now—we've found a nearby plain.

~ *Katherine Quevedo*

HETCH HETCHY

The grasses hissed beneath the oaks that mark
These fields. But now her swimming pool has spread
A net of light up into shadowed bark.
One over-irrigated oak falls dead.

Yosemite must overflow its well
And Edens drown to fill this pool, to force
A pastel wash upon an arid swell
Of chaparral. Her husband wants divorce.

She always fancied aqueducts. They reach
Across the travel album postcards she
Still keeps: through Nîmes, through Merida, through each
Brown book of empire branching to the sea.

And snaking through her garden hose, they soak
The poles that prop the last enduring oak.

~ *Eric Meub*

Palm Springs Desert Dystopia

Now is the hour the desert moon grows bright
And floats above the mountains, while its fool
Twin hides in lights that light the swimming pool,
And landscape boulders bake throughout the night,
Lit like stage props with floods of gold and pink.
The desert's hardly desert anymore:
The surest thing to come by is a drink,
And sand mostly affects a golfing score.

The Sinaloan pool man, after rain,
Finds drowned tarantulas around the drain.
He scoops them in his net and then forgets
He left them in the morning sun to dry.
After he's gone, the clumps revivify
And scatter like anarchic marionettes.

~ Leslie Monsour

TREE FALL

A season of removal settles in.
Above one ruined house—roof split in two,
a massive stump tipped forward toward a view
torn wrongly open—here the rout begins:

a harsh motet of chainsaws, metal din
ramped up by huge machinery that chews
whole trees to mulch. We wake to it, to crews
roped high, huge trunks stripped smooth as masts, and then

dismantled. And it seems a kind of cruel
collective punishment—the trees come down,
leave stark our streets, in answer to the one

whose roots gave way in Spring—but still, the rule
of fear prevails: Our precious pine, whose crown
leans high and south, must go before it's done.

~ D.R. Goodman

HIBISCUS AT THE SLIDER DOORS

It's on the cusp of its decline, each bell,
each full, lush globe of it: four yellow flowers
like nuclear blasts seen from space. Great powers
have just begun their war. This won't end well.
And here, this weekend, half the flowers and leaves
(the fat buds, too, frozen mid-bloom) will fall,
the cat squirreling them off. By first snowfall,
I'll have a potted stick. If one believes
in spring, and waters to that end, its roots
may get another year: front step, June sun—
if not, its space here will grow bleak, and one
dark rainy morning, I'll dash out in boots
to dump it by the fence. It's perfect though,
this bright. An arrogance. It doesn't know.

~ Benjamin S. Grossberg

HABITAT

In an expanse of reeds, two blackbirds nest.
One wears on either wing a scarlet patch;
One sports gold plumage on its head and breast.
Their voices, like those markings, do not match,
The yellow-head's unmusical and harsh.
When both birds seek the nesting sites they need,
Their competition subdivides the marsh:
The red-wing, marginally the smaller breed,
Must make do at the margins, while its rival
Conquers the choicer center to hold sway
Where slightly deeper water aids survival
By keeping land-based predators at bay.
Via such nuance is one habitat
Parsed into this distinctive realm and that.

~ *Chris O'Carroll*

The Velociraptor and the Protoceratops

The raptor slashes with its sickle claw;
lethal, but not itself immune from harm.
The herbivore clamps down its horn-beaked jaw,
crushing the bones of its attacker's arm.
These two are fighting to the death, of course:
no way can both of them emerge alive.
Driven by nature's most primeval force
they struggle on, but neither will survive—
there is no winner of this fateful clash.
The dune above them, waterlogged by rains,
collapses as the creatures writhe and thrash.
The irony is lost on reptile brains:
the same wet sand that smothers their last breath
will grant them immortality in death.

~ Tim Taylor

Of Soldiers and Others

Peace hath her victories no less renowned than war
—Milton, "Sonnet on General Cromwell," 1652

Of soldiers, one in five will shoot to kill,
The generals say—though any of the five
Can die. While most rise quick and fire at will,
I see the eye, the steady hand survive

And rise a crack above the barricade,
And with the firm imagination of
The bullet in the other's head once made
He holds his breath and squeezes as in love.

It's clear why Cromwell's army never lost,
For every man of his meant what he shot—
Was glad to die if that was what life cost—
Because he aimed at what he really thought.

The heart unfocused fires and takes a dive.
But loving what it loves—just one in five.

~ *Mike Carson*

MILITARY FUNERAL

The muffled roll of drums, the folded flag;
Three volleys from bolt-actions, sharp and crisp;
The clink of cartridge casings, and a wisp
Of bluish smoke. Then "Taps" begins its drag
Of lengthened notes—a melismatic wail
That seems to last forever. Next the scrape
Of boots as guardsmen exit, while black crepe
Billows beside the bier, an unlashed sail
Loose in autumnal breeze. The moment hits
The widow, whose composure starts to break.
She cannot hold back sobs; her shoulders shake.
Except for her, the grief-numbed family sits
As if held in suspended animation,
Deaf to the murmured ". . .from a grateful nation."

~ Joseph S. Salemi

ANTHEM

Do me a favor: when you go outside,
look over toward the harbor. If you squint
you'll see it—or you won't—but it can't hide
from sun, setting or rising. There's a hint,
a remnant where a spangled patch embroidered
above the rosy contrails of the dawn
still waves, as if the stars had reconnoitered
their sister light.
           Why do I ramble on?
There was a battle once to tear away
that piece of cloth and burn it while we slept.
We triumphed—but the gremlins are at play,
sowing confusion as to what we've kept
and what we're losing now unless we save
more than a recollection of the brave.

~ Claudia Gary

THE NEW OZYMANDIAS

I met a man from lands not far away,
Who said "A statue made of steel and stone
Stands ruined and half sunken in a bay
Submerged up to her waist and all alone

but holding high a single torch, a light
that may have lit her disowned land and tried
To tell the world she had dispelled the night
And welcomed everyone, no one denied.

Below the water these words still appear:
"Give me your tired, your poor" and those oppressed
Who search for safety, for escape from fear.
She would accept all those foully distressed.

Unfortunately now there's just decay
And little else in that polluted bay.

~ Mel Goldberg

OUT OF THE NIGHT

Timothy McVeigh, called the Oklahoma Bomber,
chose Henley's "Invictus" as his epitaph.

We saw your death—they showed it on TV—
and had revenge if vengeance was our goal.
You thanked the gods, whatever gods may be,
and spoke of your unconquerable soul.
We shared a god—no, not the one whose whole
existence was compassionate, who tried
by promising redemption to console
his wayward children, and was crucified.
We chose your sterner god to be our guide,
with ancient tribal precepts and a sword.
Though Hope and Charity did not abide,
Faith lived when our uncompromising Lord—
not often merciful but always just—
demanded eye for eye and dust for dust.

~ *David Gwilym Anthony*

MOSCOW ZOO

We saw the mass grave at the Moscow Zoo.
A sullen man dug up a human skull
Then held it high for journalists to view.
Forensic specialists arrived to cull
Remains and clues from this forgotten plot
On which the zoo still plans to cage a bear.
The experts guessed these prisoners were shot
For special reasons; no one was aware
Of comparable scenes at urban sites.
No one knew if these bones belonged to spies,
Suspected Jews or zealous Trotskyites,
So none of us displayed the least surprise
When bureaucrats emerged in quiet cars
To hint this might have been the work of czars.

~ A.M. Juster

Biting the Hand

My master is the one who gives me food
From little cans or out of the big bag,
And all he seems to want is gratitude,
To hear me whimper and watch my tail wag.

My master has a tempting, meaty hand
With plump fingers and greasy fingertips
That point and wiggle with each barked command
And smell like pizza and potato chips.

I want to bite it, badly, but I can't.
No. Bad doggie. I could lose everything,
My free meals, my whole living arrangement,
All for one quick nip, just to hear him sing.

Somewhere an old wolf howls on some wild hill.
I know the day is coming when I will.

~ David Stephenson

EARTHBOUND

Our injured goose can hear the wild geese cry.
They're passing over. Listening to their call
she answers. Wave on wave of them go by
to settle on the lake. Then that is all.
She seems to listen still, but who can tell?
Who knows what goes on in a goose's mind?
I can't pretend to, though at times I find
I feel as though I understand her well.

I understand she's earthbound, and not free.
Dependent, hurting, proud, not what she was:
once ruler in her realm, who used to be
Queen of the Lake, now in a cage because
of something bad that happened she can't know
while, overhead, the wild geese call, then go.

~ Bruce Bennett

Mill Valley

Today I found the body of the deer
Who used to eat my garden rose by rose.
I recognized her by the ragged ear
She flared once when I sprayed her with the hose.

Today I came across the bones again,
The curving ribs arranged in two white rows
About a wilting bush. I noticed then
The bud these ribs so piously enclose.

Today, to fit in my familiar drill
Before a business trip, I somehow rose
At five to carry water up the hill.
You'll call it an obsession, I suppose.

On coming home I found my garden piled
With leaves: how had I let it grow this wild?

~ Eric Meub

DUCK DIGNITY

I give her lettuce. She can barely move,
but manages to snatch it with her beak,
as if she still has something left to prove,
and wants that known, and lets her actions speak.
I am alive, they say. Her eyes are clear.
I'm what I always was, and I am strong.
And she will hiss if she thinks I'm too near.
Each time I've thought we've lost her I've been wrong.
I'm glad to be, but don't want her to suffer.
And so I watch and wait, which suits us fine.
I still have lots of lettuce left to offer,
and sympathy, although it's only mine.
She doesn't need it, gesture, thought, or word.
She'll take my lettuce though. Our tough old bird.

~ Bruce Bennett

Damaged Goods

On market day, my nag and I will pull
our aching selves and overburdened cart
to town, with foraged fruit and garden cull.
For there, among the peddlers taking part,
the jugglers, fools and passersby, I'll hawk
these apples, soft and fallen, scallions scorned,
these battered, stringy beans from trampled stalks,
this mildewed melon, gap-tooth ears of corn.

If just one shopper saw some value here
or stopped to bargain, she would find my fees
are low, my terms are easy. None comes near.
Once more tonight, my nag and I will feed
on foraged fruit and garden cull, our type
of damaged goods—the bruised and overripe.

~ Ted Charnley

To A Mismatched Pair: A Valentine

The teenaged couple waiting for the train
must be in love or think they are, although
his arms are not quite long enough to go
around her broad expanse, and they're both plain;
graceless, bad teeth, bad skin. Still they remain,
their bodies locked in the imperfect O
of their embrace. Uncharmed by their bold show
we look at them and look away again.

But what if they were beautiful? We'd look
and find their love a lovely thing: no flaw
would hide the content of their hearts or draw
our eyes away from such an open book—
as though we thought a photo-op emotion
could be the only measure of devotion.

~Lisa Barnett

DAREDEVIL

I started racing dirt bikes, and soon learned
That what crowds really hope for is a crash,
So being poor from racing, I soon turned
To doing sideshow stunts to earn some cash.

I specialize in high speed ramp jumps, where
You rocket over large things through the air,
Old cars mostly, but one time a caged bear,
And a retired school bus at the state fair.

The hard part's coming down. I've had some spills
And broken bikes and bones, and been laid up,
But most jumps go fine, and it pays the bills,
So I have not yet had the sense to stop;

I know it takes a heavy toll on me,
But most jobs do that, just less openly.

~ David Stephenson

III

Onset

Remember with my sitting parents I
at napkins red with cloth a table high
things struggling out to figure how these thin
(which home I knew at bags came plastic in)
potatoes were, and hamburger my how
to a connection have could any cow.

Twist change and blithely we our world: we light
and pave like soft, good day the earth, the night.
We wonder so that find what easy it
twist well ourselves as to? We still can sit
for desks behind long money hours for bland
and nation hate on any can command.

Hard shapes for make can strange it us our new
recall in shapes the which we born were to.

~ Max Gutmann

A Day in June

Sister, sister, the one I never had
spilled out of her skin. Saffron to crimson hue
shadowed the grin of silver pails; her bed,
left on log bridge through marsh, freckled with dew
like wood pillars that prop our bungalow
on still water. She, who calls for my aid
when all is dark beyond the salt wind's throe—
her throat earth-brown, her hair the twisting braid
of mangrove roots—would be woman today.
Outside our door, neighboring schoolboys chilled
by their recollections reengage to spray
the moss-scented rainwater, like what filled
vessels when she transposed beyond our house.
Mother clings to the yellowed baby blouse.

~ *Alexander Pepple*

FUGITIVE SON

The Japanese mourn children they abort.
In Shinto shrines they pick a figurine
To represent the life that they cut short.
They bow, then slide a folded note between
The sandalwood and jade as if a soul
That never loved a face could now forgive
Or any act of penance could control
Unwanted visits from a fugitive.

I never picked a message I could send
Or bargained for forgiveness. There was none.
Although I know my boy does not intend
More pain, he asks about the nameless son
We lost three months before he was conceived.
I have no words to tell him how we grieved.

~ *A.M. Juster*

Toddler Beneath a Jacaranda

Pale purple flowers, falling one by one,
strew the brick steps and sidewalk where she plays.
The wind chimes resonate in morning haze
soon to be burned to nothing by the sun.
She squats to wad some flowers in a ball,
thrusts fistfuls through a railing, lets them drop
on plush grass, smiles, and turns without a stop
to squat again—as if she'll clear them all.

Her father sits hunched over on a wall.
Protective, tired, he trains his eyes on her;
the street beyond dissolves into a blur
of trees, parked cars, and condos. In a lull,
the chimes grow still, and then he hears her sing,
in nonsense syllables, the end of spring.

~ Kevin Durkin

RECREATION

Rain gone, most houses turn out children to
the street for games which no interior
accommodates. The older kids confer
about what to play first, as well as who
gets to be captain of each team. A slew
of younger kids are chosen, him then her,
for skill if not for size. The regular
remainders shuffle toward the curbs on cue.

Inside one house one girl still sits before
the window of her room. She sees the sun
come out, disperse the clouds, then hit the floor
where rests a jigsaw puzzle nearly done.
Norman Rockwell's *The Runaway* needs ten
more pieces, so she fits them in, again.

~ *Jane Blanchard*

Fireball

At eight years old, I dodged the sisters' eyes:
ate my sandwich, then donned a saintly face,
walked out the gate, past Church and up the rise
toward Horn's Variety, that mythic place.
The path was new to me. I walked alone
and genuflected to inspect a sheared-
off branch, a mica fleck, a swallow's bone.
I used a stick to write *DAM HELL*; then cleared
away the words. Dust pleated in my skirt.
I felt a breath unloosen in my chest,
expanding, fearless in this wondrous dirt
of disobedience, this fresh unrest.
The church bells rang. I rose, denied the call.
Picked freedom, sin, a red hot Fireball.

~ Kyle Potvin

COUNTERFEITER

Inside a diary quite pink and tame,
in purple ink my first love's name was set.
But I was nine, so names renounced became
confetti I could scatter and forget.
Compelled to purge each scrap of evidence,
I ripped. The rabbit on the cover smiled,
more willing to be marred by this offense
than by these false devotions be defiled.

I grew, pronounced my love upon men's lips
in earnest. Feathery, each stroke I signed,
my body scrawled across the mattress. Script
so deftly forged leaves volumes to unbind.
And now, mind stained with my calligraphy,
what can I tear with schoolgirl luxury?

~ Nicole Caruso Garcia

No Bloody Way!

for Mark and Mike, whose room it was

A crowd of students sitting round a room
One summer night in 1983.
They barely move, make little sound, assume
They've every right to simply wait and see.
Until the college porter comes along
To tell them that they're threatening the peace.
It's obvious he's got his sums all wrong.
And what's he going to do? Ring the police?

This memory will always ebb and flow;
A part of me has still to come of age.
So when, today, I find a treble "No!"
Means rattling the same old bloody cage,
I'm back in Oxford sounding out success,
The silent choir inside me shouting "Yes!"

~ *Duncan Gillies MacLaurin*

Life Drawing

for Meredith Bergmann

Professor Z. laughed at my first male nude.
The proportions weren't classical; he thought
the true-to-life sized genitals were lewd.
"No, not like *that*," he said. "Here's what you ought
to do." He took my chalk and sketched a shape
inside the one I'd drawn. I thought, high school,
where artists' models must be dressed or draped
with no exception. Modest was the rule.
I wondered if Professor Z. approved
of students drawing what they cannot see,
if he liked pictures with the truth removed.
His act brought out the stubborn side of me,
so I erased his marks upon the figure,
and then I made the private parts much bigger.

~Lisa Barnett

108

CHESS WITH MONSIEUR JOFFROY

in memory of Frédérique Joffroy, 1962-1980

To lose to me was not the badge of shame
Your father thought it was; he couldn't stop
The stronger player coming out on top.
It stung me royally to hear him claim
My proletarian tactics were to blame.
It's standard stuff to snatch a pawn, then swap
Off everything; slow suicide to drop
The basic principle behind the game.
To think that he was meant to be the host!
We were thirteen, your father forty-four.
Five years later I was told, by post,
That you, my friend, had hanged yourself. Your ghost
Jolted my memory. Outplayed once more,
Your father kicked the table to the floor.

~ *Duncan Gillies MacLaurin*

On Getting a Record Player For Christmas

It comes right back, that old familiar move.
I lift the needle, use my fingertip,
And set it down exactly in the groove—
Can't drop it or it makes the record skip.

The notes call up a scene inside my head,
My bedroom, where I'd listened to that song:
Red lamp, some flowered curtains, low twin bed,
The mirror where I'd always sing along.

And then what I remember most of all:
Between songs, quiet filled with so much sound—
The hum of the machine, the rhythmic scrawl
Of the wavy record slowly turning round.

I memorized not only every word,
But all the scratchy silences I heard.

~ Midge Goldberg

THE BIG SMOKE

for Will

We took a flat in central Hammersmith—
Both students, we were working several nights
At some hotel— amboozled by the myth
Of being where it's at. We scorned the sights
We never saw. The day you said you'd scored,
I thought you meant a girl, not Mary Jane,
Yet I too fell beneath her spell. We bored
Of books and, in our loneliness and pain,
Mistook the kindness of a nurse that smiled
For promises of love, too blind to see
Our heroine was nothing but a child
That stroked the ego till it proved to be
Collapsible—a folding carry-cot
She jubilantly folded, then forgot.

~ *Duncan Gillies MacLaurin*

Elegy For a Preschool Teacher

When feeling shy, my daughter held her hand
and calmly watched the other children play.
A swing's chain squeaked, a shovel scraped the sand,
but they stood silent, happiest that way.
Later, inside, she'd teach the class a song
about a beauty charmed to sleep, which they
would chant while she'd conduct or clap along.
Who had the most fun? Difficult to say.

The teacher had no children of her own,
but ours were hers as long as she could teach,
and though death's potion seeped into her bone,
it lacked the power to keep love out of reach.
Some nights she came in dreams to be their friend
and smiled as though their play would never end.

~ Kevin Durkin

TALKING TO LORD NEWBOROUGH

Lt. William Charles Wynn, 1873-1916, 4th Baron Newborough,
whose grave overlooks the Vale of Ffestiniog in North Wales

I'd perch beside your gravestone years ago,
a boy who thought you old at forty-three.
I knew you loved this quiet place, like me.
We'd gaze towards Maentwrog far below,
kindred spirits, and I'd talk to you.
Sometimes I asked what it was like to die—
were you afraid? You never did reply,
but silence rested lightly on us two.
These days the past is nearer, so I came
to our remembered refuge on the hill,
expecting change yet finding little there:
my village and the Moelwyns look the same,
Saint Michael's Church commands the valley still—
but you, old friend, are younger than you were.

~ *David Gwilym Anthony*

LISA LEAVING

for Lisa Lind Dunbar

For me at least, you'll always be the child
Who hated school; now never to return.
No longer need you struggle in your seat;
You're free to go; you'll soon be running wild,
Down to the sea, the sand beneath your feet,
No morons shouting: "Won't you ever learn?"

I'll miss your Scottish accent, miss your face,
Miss most your easy wit and plucky grace.
I yell: "Hey, Lisa! Leaving us for good?
You made it through! I always knew you would!
God tur! Have fun! Take care!" Defying care,
You climb King Christian's horse on Esbjerg Square,
Broad-grin at all the others fading fast,
Then ride like hell into the distant past.

~ *Duncan Gillies MacLaurin*

FATHER OF THE MAN

While wandering the borders of my mind,
uncertain where the hazy pathways led
and frightened by the darkness up ahead,
I saw my Youth approaching from behind
and paused and waited, thinking what to say.
We'd broken contact many years ago—
we hadn't much in common. Even so
his certainty might help me find the way.

He came to meet me coldly with a frown,
and I fell silent, angered, filled with such
resentment that this parent asked so much,
mixed with regret because I'd let him down.

So burdened by the weight of wasted days
I left him and we went our separate ways.

~ David Gwilym Anthony

WALKING WITH A DAUGHTER IN MY ARMS

Breathtaking women, who'd avoid my eye
if I were walking home alone, swing by
to have a chat and let me look my fill.
Even at night, they're lured against their will
to cross the street, drawn by her coos and sighs.
They share their warmest smiles, but I've grown wise:
Leaning down close, they want their fingers held
by tiny fingers; I step back, compelled
instinctively to break the tête-à-tête
before my daughter turns her face, upset.
Not used to being disappointed, they
resort to compliments and stalk away.
Teased by their fragrances, I watch them go.
My younger self would not have wished it so.

~ Kevin Durkin

ASTROLABE

Son of Abelard and Heloise

Is that a name to give your only son?
What did you care? My mother loved you so
She threw off beauty and became a nun
Only because you said, "It's over. Go,
You bride of Christ, we're only siblings now."
I never saw you save by fits and starts
And poor relations raised me, God knows how—
In wedlock born, a bastard in your hearts.
True, mother found me a small benefice
Which kept me in the church, and therefore near
To her, but never near enough to kiss,
Or talk with no one else to overhear.
Her love, your life, remained a world apart.
It took the pair of you to break my heart.

~ *Gail White*

The End

They thought they'd save themselves some grief by not
Advising us of what they had to do.
Our mother picked us up from school, her cue
To tell us our young Labrador, who'd got
A taste for blood, it seemed, had just been shot.
And when I saw that everything was true,
I felt I'd been betrayed. My parents knew
That Gail was going to die and hatched a plot
That left us out. I'm sitting in that car
In Bridge of Weir. I'm six. No sparkling wine,
No girl, no miracle, no lucky star
Will ever mitigate or redefine
That bitter blow, or extirpate the scar:
June, Friday 13th, 1969.

~ Duncan Gillies MacLaurin

THREE KINGS DAY

I should unwind the beads and twinkle-lights
but here I sit without the will to start
the packing up, the putting back. This part
I've never liked, my version of last rites.

It's January 6th, well past the day
you would have stripped the drying limbs of cheer.

The ornaments you gave me year by year,
Victorian lace fans, cream bows, gold sleigh,
reflect a mother/daughter history.
White-washed perhaps: no war, just peace—

                    Well planned!
I sense your otherworldly sleight of hand
(You led me right to this epiphany).

I linger near and sip your favorite tea.
I swear I hear you hum *O Christmas Tree.*

                    ~ Kyle Potvin

A FATHER IS A LOVER'S OPPOSITE

A father is a lover's opposite.
Each gift I've ever given you has won
for me, me, me a thing you've felt or done
that's blossomed far beyond repaying it;
the many things I give our children, though,
can never bring me any such return:
I only get to watch them grow and learn
and, very soon, when we most love them, go.
Could any states reflect each other less?
What nonsense could help Nature to explain;
how could my reaching out for such a gain
directly lead to such unselfishness?
I'm selfish still. I give to children who
are me—raised up by being mixed with you.

~ *Max Gutmann*

GOLDEN GLOVES

My father fought in Golden Gloves. Back then
The ring was where you slugged your way to hopes.
It was no place for fey, aesthetic men—
There's no nuance on canvas, or the ropes.

I asked him, *Dad, what does it mean to lace
Into someone?* He smiled, as if unpacking
An old valise of thoughts on how his face
Received its crisscrossed road map of shellacking.

*You lace into a fighter when you hit
And let your inside glove glance off his skin.
The lacing on your gloves is coarse as grit,
And cuts flesh like a file biting in.
Do it enough, his blood will start to flow.
They'll stop the fight—you'll win by TKO.*

~ *Joseph S. Salemi*

THE ROARING

The wind pulled at his hair, the cold spray stung
his brow, the sand blew in his eyes—and this
felt just right for a fool like him, who'd flung
his last chance past the breakers; an abyss
as deep as any ocean soon would claim
what future he had left. He heard derision
in crashing waves that seemed to roar his name,
condemning him and his reckless decision.
Who knew the ocean would be so unkind,
would salt regrets, leave rages newly stirred?
Enough. He went home, left the sea behind,
and poured himself the liquid he preferred.
He drank some scotch, then stumbled off to bed,
but he still heard the roaring in his head.

~ *Jean L. Kreiling*

THE FATHER

A crippled mind will always smell the limes
from daiquiris it pilfered in its youth.
My company had moved me from Duluth
along with Fred. "Ah Dad, we've heard the chimes
at midnight," says he, quoting Shakespeare, rhymes
and all. Myself, I never drink Vermouth.
Perhaps before a meal. Are you a sleuth?
I think I'd like to slap his face sometimes.

All right. What did he do? He killed a cat.
"That's all?" you say. You haven't heard it all.
He trapped it in a basket in the hall,
then skewered it and blamed it all on Nat.
I got the back brush and we had a chat.
I blame it on the stolen alcohol.

~ John J. Brugaletta

PSYCHOMYTHIC MIRROR

Your father, dark: Carpathian or Sioux.
But in this mirror, slash of shadows, you
look more like Beowulf or Hamlet: blue-
spruce eyes, with skin a northern glacial hue.
A ghost. Hurt hunter born to die. Or dread
prince sacrificed, come back to life. You're pitched
too high for the quotidian, you've ditched
the baggage of the dollar, drunk and fed
on honey-dew, on milk of paradise.
Existence in your world cannot sustain
itself except in flux: clouds torn, black ice
quicksilvered by the sun, red lava plain,
a dark core throbbing rays of light that slice
old wounds like moons bleed tides of bliss and pain.

~ Thomas Zimmerman

AGAIN TODAY

Again today you perk up at the news
That I'm your son, which comes as a surprise
Again today. I watch the smile suffuse
Your face and lift the pained fog from your eyes.
That cloudy grimace of anxiety,
A blank, bewildered everything's-gone-wrong,
Disperses as you hug and laugh with me.
You've lost your grip, but your embrace is strong.
The fog will roll back in. Tomorrow we
Will play one more revival of this show,
The same confusion, same discovery.
You'll learn again that I'm someone you know,
We'll clasp again this interlude of joy,
Then you'll let go, again, of your lost boy.

~ Chris O'Carroll

NOT HOME

Her window framed midwinter darkness traced
with feathered frost. Half-slumped in her white gown—
my father's arms secure around her waist,
her bare feet on his shoes, her eyes cast down—
she swung, submissive, to the brass and bass
piped through a speaker in the corridor
and kept on plucking at her yellowed lace
as if at a corsage that she once wore.

"Johnny," she said, her first word of the night,
her husband's name. "Oh, John, where have you been?"
"I'm Jim," her son replied, as their slow spin
concluded near her bed. The nightstand light
bathed her divided lenses with its gold
and filled with shadow every crease and fold.

~ Kevin Durkin

LATE LAST NIGHT

she penciled animals with her left hand:
dark pigs and dogs, but "Horses are too hard,"
she said. Self-conscious, with a diamond band,
a tight red dress, a round face acne-scarred,
she had bad teeth because she only brushed
the fronts. She kissed me. I smelled cigarettes,
her Heraclitean fire. Such moods! Blue-hushed,
to black, to blacker yet . . . a thousand *yet*s.
And yet, she said she loved me: "You're a good
man, just a little rough around the edge."
I pledged that I'd live wilder if I could.
And then the moon above the cedar hedge . . .
so white it blinded me till pale daylight.
I dreamed of my dead mother late last night.

~ *Thomas Zimmerman*

What Remains

He feels her absence, though, all the time. He understands now.
Our absence is what remains of us.
　　—Catherine O'Flynn, The News Where You Are

What will remain of you? What is the shape
your absence will impress on those who've known
your presence? A familiar void will gape,
its haunting silhouette and style your own.
Someone will reach out for your hand and find
your bony knuckles are no longer there;
a lack of laughing blue eyes will remind
someone of yours. When you fail to prepare
the one dessert that Uncle Fred will eat,
when gardens you once tended fail to bloom,
when crossword puzzles are left incomplete,
it's possible another might assume
your roles, but not the way you did, for no
replacement quite fills your shape when you go.

~ *Jean L. Kreiling*

MATURING

Each day means fewer things that he can do.
Some years ago he lost his sense of smell,
and now he hardly bends to tie his shoe.

You understand. I'm sure that you can tell
he's getting old; he's edging toward his grave.
Slave traders aren't enticed. He wouldn't sell.

I won't say he is cowardly or brave—
he's just uninterested in pain or fear.
He's lived from birth inside a verbal cave.

But now his heart is shrunk, his eyes are blear,
and he has seen some things he'll never say,
except by tangents, to his biosphere.

One thing he still delights in is to play
while kneeling with a child as if he'd pray.

~ John J. Brugaletta

FORBIDDING FRUIT

Resigned to wheelchair life, too weak to stand,
She cursed her body, calling it a hearse.
The family stopped eating from her hand
The day she put her mortgage in reverse.
Likewise, her mood regressed from foul to worse:
Restricted diet, ill-prepared and bland,
The mortifying mop-ups by the nurse—
She killed a kind word with a reprimand.

Still, fleeting joy could take her by surprise,
As when she bit into that Bartlett pear:
Sweet recognition danced across her eyes,
Glad juice spilled down her cheek into her hair.
She held the bitten fruit out like a prize
That none, not one of us, wanted to share.

~ Leslie Monsour

The Hard Work of Dying

The hospice nurse explained the letting go.
Give her space to do the work of dying.
On the sill, a green heirloom tomato,
brought in before the frost, sat there, sighing.
Or was that me, not knowing what to say?
Don't ask her things (such grief in giving up
exchanges!). *Back off engagement*—that way
we help her go. Tea grows cold in my cup.
Ten days since Emma took a sip of tea
or ate a slice of grape. She sleeps while rain
whispers a soothing chatter. The oak tree
clears its throat, weeping acorns in the drain.
Yellow snapdragons brighten up the room.
A day from now they'll see a second bloom.

~ *Kyle Potvin*

CANCER PRAYER

Dear Lord,

        Please flood her nerves with sedatives
and keep her strong enough to crack a smile
so disbelieving friends and relatives
can temporarily sustain denial.

Please smite that intern in oncology
who craves approval from department heads.

Please ease her urge to vomit; let there be
kind but flirtatious men in nearby beds.

Given her hair, consider amnesty
for sins of vanity; make mirrors vanish.

Surround her with forgiving family
and nurses not too numb to cry. Please banish
trite consolations; take her in one swift
and gentle motion as your final gift.

~ A.M. Juster

TELLING TIME

The clock face lies. It shows a paltry round
of just twelve hours between her bleary-eyed
awaking—when she still expects the sound
of his damp, raspy breathing at her side—
and dinnertime, when she will set the table
with just one placemat, one fork, and one plate,
and reheat last night's casserole. What fable
pretends her loneliness does not inflate
each minute into an eternity,
the neatly measured day's duration swelling
until she can't tell time? In tragedy,
it's always time itself that does the telling,
the story circular: a grim cliché
retold in twelve long chapters twice a day.

~ *Jean L. Kreiling*

ANECDOTAL EVIDENCE

My aunt who brought her kidney function back
by eating grapefruit seeds for fifty days
makes no impression on our local quack.
It's anecdotal evidence, he says.
There are no reproducible results.
Another person might eat grapefruit seeds
for fifty days and cease to have a pulse.
Cause and effect's the evidence he needs.

The evidence is all in favor of
the proposition that the dead are dead,
despite our bitter hope and wistful love.
Yet when my mother died, my father said
that just before the chill that would not thaw,
her face lit up with joy at what she saw.

~ *Gail White*

PROTOCOL

"Does my wife need to be here?"

The question makes me laugh, but not out loud.
I do not want to bother those around,
especially other patients, each avowed
to victory. A nurse starts to expound
the risks of chemotherapy, but you
soon point to me and learn my company
is optional. I know just what to do:
after today grant you the liberty
of driving here and sitting here to get
the special intravenous cocktail no
one else can share. Why should I be upset?
To keep you longer, I must let you go,
as you prefer, on Mondays, all alone—
then wait for messages from your smartphone.

~ *Jane Blanchard*

An Absence

No one can cry forever, and the world
we live in thinks our grief should be discreet,
not violent like a pitcher's fast ball hurled
into the stands. Our culture favors neat
solutions—counseling, group therapy,
physical workouts, nothing from the gut,
all head-work—lacking the simplicity
of cures for cancer: poison, burn, and cut.
I wouldn't disappoint my friends—who care
what happens next, whose expectations are
that I'll move forward, more or less the same.
I give no trouble, having learned to bear
my loss of you well-covered, like the scar
that was a breast before the surgeons came.

~ *Gail White*

On the Suicide of a Friend

God help the kids! I heard the neighbours say—
so quick to judge, though mostly they were kind.
They saw the sorry mess you left behind
and thought you took the coward's selfish way.

The coward's way? No, not that I can see:
despair's a snare. They say a fox will gnaw
its fettered limb and sacrifice the paw:
what desperation drove you to break free?

Nor were you selfish. Just beneath the calm
the darkness gathered; I have known it too.
It touched the ones you loved: I'm certain you
believed you were protecting them from harm.

God—if there is a God—will grant you rest:
you failed, we all do, but you did your best.

~ *David Gwilym Anthony*

No

No, not this time. I cannot celebrate
a man's discarded life, and will not try;
these knee-jerk elegies perpetrate
Plath's nightshade lies. Why should we glorify
descent into a solipsistic hell?
Stop. Softly curse the waste. Don't elevate
his suffering to genius. Never tell
me he will live on. Never call it fate.

Attend the service. Mourn. Pray. Comfort those
he lacerated. Keep him in your heart,
but use that grief to teach. When you compose
a line, it is a message, not just art.
Be furious with me, but I refuse
to praise him. No, we have too much to lose.

~ A.M. Juster

KITTY

Sweet friendly pills, you never once complain,
But nestle in your alabaster urn
Behind the jewelry box and the Guerlain.
One night, angelic host, you'll have your turn.

My *vanity:* the word's a commonplace.
I used to give philosophy a pass,
But every morning now I rise to face
Ecclesiastes peering from my glass.

The ruin of allure is hardly kind.
How can Miss Austen, though, have nothing more
To say of little sisters left behind?
Where are the chapters we were waiting for?

My little pills, a little gravity
Will root me to the landscape, like a tree.

~ *Eric Meub*

IV

THE HOTEL ROOM

He wouldn't call, and that would be her clue,
announcement-making not among his skills.
He flared that whole first conference day in Rome.
New freedom loomed, the nearest of the hills;
the prism that he saw the city through,
it blotted any thought at all of home,
swelling him like a wallet thick with bills.
But entering his room at the hotel,
the curtains drawn, the shaded lamplight dim,
the thin-legged table pushed against the wall,
the solitary bed, its quilt smoothed well
by bored and unseen hands, for one like him,
the feeling, with a dizzy swiftness, fell.
He had to hear her voice, and made the call.

~ Max Gutmann

The Spirit Changes

The spirit changes. Sometimes in the shock
of altered circumstance—just to survive.
The mind adjusts. The heart, wanting to live—
endures, that is—unrusts the frozen lock
you thought would never give. A gate swings through;
in place of grief, new possibility.
Like *that*. As though the heart and mind agree
to dial the world a few degrees askew
and call it normal. Sometimes, though, the dial
just slips—adaptive power becomes a kind
of glitch. You waken on the other shore,
the ocean to your left, your path a mile
off course—but you don't question what you find.
You think you just don't love him anymore.

~ *D.R. Goodman*

WOMAN AT CLOTHESLINE

after the painting by Alex Colville

I won't wait until all the laundry's dried;
it doesn't matter that my basket's not
quite full and more hangs on the line. Inside,
he's watching golf on TV—hasn't got
a clue about my plans, what else I bear
besides clean sheets, or even where I'll be
by lunchtime. Once more I'll walk past his chair
to make our bed with laundered linens; he
won't notice, but I like things neat. He's blind
to so much—like the slim dark dress I'm wearing,
not suitable for chores, but more the kind
you wear for travel—and he's well past caring.
But when these strappy shoes bear me away,
he'll notice he's been served no lunch today.

~ *Jean L. Kreiling*

Sonnet For Her Husband

Her husband's solid presence has to bear
the weight of shopping lists and auto rust
and gunfire on the news. Because he's there,
he's coated with a film of daily dust,
while my spruce form, if conjured up, can dwell
in moments: in the concert green remark
that made her laugh so hard, my lousy cooking
(that burnt lasagna), skating in the park,
that love-bite when her roommate wasn't looking.
Oh, substance has its perquisites—I well
remember them. But daily living grinds
their sharpest colors down. Our love's more suited
to growing steadily in distant minds
less real, less thought-about, and less diluted.

~ *Max Gutmann*

144

MEETING YOU AGAIN

Your face does not forget the bitter past.
'Here are my wounds,' it says, 'this is my blood'
—those laser eyes would burn me if they could,
your pleasantries are laced with broken glass.
But I say some things were not meant to last.
All changes once that truth is understood.
An early end awaits the greatest good,
the brightest flame will always burn too fast.
I suffered too, you know—here are my scars.
I wear them not with anger but with pride,
mementoes of that wild white-water ride,
earth-shaking, epoch-making love of ours.
Far better than pale lives we might have had
it had to end: it would have sent us mad.

~ *Tim Taylor*

Love Recidivus

Whatever it may be, we may suppose
it is not love, for love must leave its trace
like contraband seized and displayed in rows;
is not sufficient reason to erase
the careful lives we have so far lived through—
there is no call for us to undermine
the walls we've built; no need to think anew
of all the chains and choices that define

us still. And yet for all our fine intent
a single touch ignites the night and tries
resolve past all resisting. What we meant
before we mean again; fidelities
have yet been known to shift and come undone
and all good reasons fail us, one by one.

~Lisa Barnett

THE RAFT

Each breath a splinter, how I dreamt of land.
Below the spooling stars, a man cried out.
My fever grasped at echoes for his hand.
To my companion I became devout
and wound around him like a tourniquet.
My legs were threads of jute; half-hitches moored
him, though the sea had thrashed his silhouette.
And over time, some wounds the salt air cured.
Naïve, I thought that we would find true north,
two separate wrecks more tethered by each kiss.
But winds unstitched my oath, and drifting forth,
I let him sink beneath the green abyss;
for what I'd clung to while delirious
was never love, but something gangrenous.

~ *Nicole Caruso Garcia*

Release

You question me with patient tenderness.
"I'm fine," I lie: my leaden undertones
reveal what language struggles to express.
This sullen murk that seeps into my bones:
I have no name for it, nor has it shape
or substance. Stagnant, undefined, it sits
in hidden pools from which there's no escape.
It is my prisoner, as I am its.
But do not cease to ask: for you, each day
I try once more to picture it in words.
If I could make it concrete, find some way
to form it in the semblance of a bird
and, through the gift of wings, to set it free
then it would lift its cold embrace from me.

~ *Tim Taylor*

STYLIST

I trailed through cavern after cavern hung
With clouds of crystal from a painted sky,
And gawked at fountains on the lawn, a young
Suburban girl bewildered by Versailles.

I saw my parents didn't live this way;
And now my husband's taste—not regal, we've
Discerned. And yet that morning of parquet
Still whispers glamour, and I still believe.

Until this afternoon. I don't know why.
Perhaps because we had another fight,
Or maybe I expected more from my
IKEA kitchen. Nothing's ever right.

The guided tour, it seems, must finally stop,
If only at a granite countertop.

~ *Eric Meub*

Sanctuary

Most of the time we have no company
besides ourselves, and that is fine with us.
Now older, we are disinclined to fuss
about impressing anyone. We see
dust fall, wipe it away eventually.
It falls again, gives little stimulus
for ready action. Island life is thus
a long vacation from efficiency.

We let the nicer glassware get opaque,
the sterling silver tarnish. We permit
some sand inside, allow a residue
of salt or soap wherever. Still, I make
the bed each day for custom's benefit.
You marvel at the ocean's changing hue.

~ *Jane Blanchard*

A Girl Like You

I fantasize you're having an affair,
now that you're living with a man I hate.
He gets suspicious when you come home late,
then thinks of all the times you were not there.
Confronts you. You are ready. You deny
all allegations. Everything goes well.
He's still suspicious, but he cannot tell
for sure. He's onto you. He knows you lie,
knows you are capable of gross deceit.
He'll catch you one day. You are going to pay!
He knows you know you'll need to be discreet,
but he'll outwit you. He will find a way.
Meanwhile, the other guy, without a clue,
floats in his heaven: "Wow! A girl like you!"

~ *Bruce Bennett*

SURPRISE PARTY

Her current flame has given her a vase.
A vase. She spreads a smile across her face.
She gasps and gushes at the thing too long.
It's bright, exuberant, completely wrong.

A former love extends the gift he's found—
Somehow!—an octavo of Milton, bound
In red morocco. It's an ancient book.
She's too aglow to dare return his look.

He lifts the vase, then quickly puts it down
As if to say she's bedding with a clown.
The clown himself can't fail to realize
That brief, but errant, rapture in her eyes.

Surprise! Perhaps next time he won't insist
On managing the invitation list.

~ Eric Meub

SOLACE

I loved that ragged dog, but when the stuff
of him began to fleck my mother's floor
with bits of rubber foam, she said *enough*
and put the nasty thing behind a door
I couldn't reach. In dreams I drag a stool
across the years to pull my solace down,
and holding him I know I've been a fool
to wait this long—his rescue is my own.

So when you came that winter night, your fur
boots dragging snow, cold air, a distant wife,
I never stopped. I never thought of her
or the mess you would trail across my life.
I only saw what comfort it would be
to pull your comfort down on top of me.

~ *Debra Wierenga*

PHONOGRAPH

Remember, dear, when this was the one way
to make a disk sing? Full-size, not compact—
and both the disk and player would obey
only if you possessed your share of tact:
You'd lift the tone arm, puff a bit of air
across its fragile needle to remove
new dust, or use a brush of sable hair
to coax it out. After each vinyl groove
was polished with the softest chamois cloth,
you'd spin a record on its table, place
the needle over it, light as a moth—
you must remember! For the way you trace
the path of every melody I store
shows gentleness I've never known before.

~ *Claudia Gary*

THE GIST OF IT

I heard you one time laughing on the phone,
but did not catch the gist of it, just then.
It was about your juggling different men.
That's when I thought that you were mine alone.
I must have felt it somehow was a joke,
or I misheard. How could you just assume
that casual tone when I was in the room
and clearly overhearing what you spoke?
Oh, afterwards I put it all together.
You *wanted* me to hear. You thought it quaint
to offer me that chance to be a saint,
teased and tormented by the choice of whether
to call you on your boldness, or accept
the harsh conditions on which I'd be kept.

~ Bruce Bennett

Nobody's Perfect

Nobody's perfect. Now and then, my pet,
You're almost human. You could make it yet.
    —from Wendy Cope's sonnet, "Faint Praise"

In Wendy Cope's "Faint Praise," she makes the case
Her current lover's not quite up to snuff.
It's clear she thinks that faint praise is enough,
And doesn't even say it to his face.
Let's hear it for faint praise. It's not that bad,
And often is the most that one can get.
Consider this. Would you be *less* upset
With no praise? Surely not. One should be glad
To have one's love give any praise at all,
even if it *is* scant and insincere.
Or, say there *is* no praise, you still can hear
That praise that could have been, which will forestall
That moment when it will be clear as day
That she'd prefer that you just go away.

~ *Bruce Bennett*

156

Snow White's Plea to the Huntsman

Asleep, I shiver in a silken gown
and wait for you to find me in the dark.
Don't let me waken shackled to a crown,
too drowsy to resist that royal mark.
You saved me once and fooled the wicked queen
who craved a lung and liver fricassee.
Though served a hoax, she licked her fingers clean.
By sparing me your sword, you captured me.
Let moonlight vigil lead you to my lips,
and prove your kiss will break this spell's embrace.
The prickly arrows of your cheek eclipse
affection from the smoothest princely face.
Such knaves can plunder castles, trinkets, art,
but only you can breach my fortressed heart.

~ *Nicole Caruso Garcia*

ME

It's true, Lake Lagunitas sparkles like
The windows at Bulgari, but, as I've
Remarked before, you idolize your hike,
Why can't I idolize Rodeo Drive?

And I agree, a giant redwood has
An urban grandeur, and in spite of fog,
Sonoma and Marin are pretty as
The latest Crate & Barrel catalogue.

But while the woods may be a match for, say,
A crowded Music Center symphony,
The difference is, your trees (unlike LA)
Aren't equally impressed by perfect *me*.

Imagine the safaris I can buy us.
Just let me be, for once, your Tamalpais.

~ Eric Meub

No Love Lost

Love's never lost, but only stowed away
In darkened atria; it pulses there
Unmarked, not quite forgotten. We're aware
Of flutters now and then, but cannot say
Just what the cause—a sound, a certain play
Of light that pleases, or a smoky air
Of possibility—a wisp is there
And gone, too thin to grasp. And then one day,
Capriciously, it spills as if on cue
Into an ordinary world of streets
And littered crosswalks, where a girl in blue
Tight denim strides, black muscle shirt, slick part
And chiseled, boyish look, and almost meets
The old unguarded gaze of my changed heart.

~ D.R. Goodman

BLACKBERRYING

It's Eden; no male gamete needed here.
Wet flowers drop their petals. Ovaries,
Self-fertilized, swell. Pericarps appear
Around dense seeds, flesh thickens, spring's green tease

Blushed red expands, this ripened purple pull
A virgin birth of juicy, sweet-dark fruit
I'm picking warm. I've filled three buckets full,
Lush brambles wildly spreading, taking root

All through the garden, arching branches stretch
Halfway across the driveway, subtle scent
Of blossoms giving way to heady fetch
Of blackberry seductions. Hours I've spent

Through sticky scratch of thorns, and borne this fleet
Communion in my sweaty hands. Take, eat.

~ Beth Houston

LOVESICK SONNET #2

You're kissing, in each other's arms: it's world
enough. And time? You've stopped it: history
is past—and tense, as usual. It's hurled
clay on the potter's wheel. The mystery?
Its center cannot hold. All things, they fall
apart. It's entropy as destiny.
Not now, however. Loving words forestall
such endings: "You bring out the best in me."
"It tingles everywhere you touch." There's not
much sense in stats or consequences. Yes,
effects will have their cause. But bodies ought
to *breathe* in tombs: sea-change survivors bless
instead of grieve. Your love, it never sickens,
as even in dead earth, fresh new life quickens.

~ *Thomas Zimmerman*

DESIRES ARE INTERCHANGEABLE

Desires are interchangeable. Take thirst:
A primal craving, surely; yet I pass
Your door en route, and wanting in the worst
Way just to quench my arid tongue, I cross
The threshold, and drink you, instead, for hours.
Take hunger: this sensation at my core
Is plain and physical—and yet your powers
Of interplay will fill me till no more
Can enter, nor is wanted. And take greed:
My taste for fine possessions, which I keep
Like treasures, has been traded for a need
Of everything that's yours. And then, take sleep:
    I've found in waking all that rest requires—
    These dreams of you, these surfeited desires.

~ D.R. Goodman

The Gift

Some days, we fly apart: The words won't come.
The head's unscrewed. The limbs so loose, unstrung,
we're piecemeal puppets. Pipes are shot, the plumb-
line's snapped. Our body rags flap twisted, wrung
like tattered flags on some accursed field,
the sodden earth a mill, a churn, a maw
devouring all we think we are. But caw
of crow, of crone, can raise a sun fresh-peeled,
moon's revenant. A string quartet, a mad
sonata licking wounds, a spell cast wrong
that knits and doesn't snag the wild and free
synaptic sparking in the brain, the bong
exhausted, tinctures chugged, and we, charmed we,
reclaim the gift, the song we've always had.

~ *Thomas Zimmerman*

SPOUSES WHO FIGHT LIVE LONGER

title from a LiveScience.com headline

Shall I compare thee to a pugilist
With butterfly's bright float, bee's brighter sting?
We never vowed we never would get pissed
Enough for heated rounds inside this ring.
To be one flesh and yet not of one mind
Can lead to clamming up or thrashing out;
The latter, all the research seems to find,
Is better for longevity. No doubt
We both have opened wounds we should repent,
Have landed verbal barbs with too sure aim,
But the aerobic vim with which we vent
Feeds oxygen to love's enduring flame.
So long as eyes can flash and breath come fast,
So long may this close-quarters combat last.

~ Chris O'Carroll

HEATHCLIFF

I'd say, "I'm Heathcliff." You would laugh. "You're not."
I really felt the dark and brooding love
consuming and possessing me was what
compelled our course. Oh, I was conscious of
its silliness, its danger; all the rest,
but still, you were the center and the whole.
You ruled my every breath; I was obsessed.
No more myself, my self had no control,
or so I thought, and said. You took it well,
though with that teasing smile. How could I know
of shadowy subplots that you would not tell?
Dark secret places where I could not go?
I see now all those clues I did not see.
Yes, you knew Heathcliff, and he was not me.

~ Bruce Bennett

Mass Mailing Invitation

You know the sort—the postcard that gets stuck
between the ads for siding and the plea
for missing children, that you usually
toss out, more rubbish for the garbage truck.

But, inadvertently, one day, you pluck
the invitation out, and go, and he
and you first meet. You just as easily
might not have met, a simple case of luck:

enough to send you screaming to the skies
about the crazy vagaries of it all,
everything resting on a thing so small,

the million chances you don't recognize
much less take, and then, the one you took—
the random blessedness of that one look.

~ *Midge Goldberg*

166

Unspace

It is the gap that severs what is said
from what is understood. The hidden place
where thoughts ferment: they say "inside the head"
but such things are not to be found in space
of three dimensions: nor indeed could we
mark out in feet and inches the abyss
that time has opened between you and me.
Hope tells me I could bridge it with a kiss,
so near are we in space: I hear your heart
and feel your breath upon my skin, and yet
in unspace, we're a universe apart,
beyond the reach of healing or regret.
Sensing your sadness, I reach out to cross
but fall into the chasm, and am lost.

~ *Tim Taylor*

REGRET

"Inopem me copia fecit." Wealth has left me empty-handed.
—*Ovid,* Metamorphoses

In retrospect, I never thought I'd get
To wrap my hand around your naked breast
Until your boyfriend's timely absence blessed
Our secret love. You begged me not to fret,
Insisted that your boyfriend was no threat,
Till I believed your leaving him was best
For everyone. And neither of us guessed
We'd each in turn be ravaged by regret.
A heavy price for such a petty theft.
Admittedly, we could have been more deft.
I waited seven weeks for you to call.
Your valentine arrived too late; I'd left
For Italy. Quite innocent, I'd fall
For someone else. I meant no harm at all.

~ *Duncan Gillies MacLaurin*

168

OUR LETTERS

They may be smudged, delayed, misunderstood,
redundant, mangled, undelivered, lost,
or contradictory. They may have crossed
each other in some sketchy neighborhood.
Their narratives may falter where they could
have raced ahead. We may have crumpled, tossed,
and inked them yet again at unknown cost
of perseverance, sleep, or firewood
until, resigned to what we have revealed,
we trust they will eventually arrive
where we've always imagined them to be—
in front of one another's eyes, unsealed
to say, "Without you I am still alive,
but barely." And to hope that you agree.

~ *Claudia Gary*

LOVE SONNET

My love is like the Shostakovich Pre-
Ludes Opus 34, his melody
A lilting line that spins and slips away
To reappear behind a minor key,
Or tangled in the cord that lifts the blinds
Upon a bright, chromatic city view—
Or dark and brooding night—whate'er he finds
Is made a dance: Waltz of a Drunken Crew,
Three-Legged Polka—joyous dissonance
In sudden tantrums of hilarity,
Then liquid measures of sweet resonance
And tonic depth—a wild complexity
Of twenty-four dimensions, half above
And half below G-flat: Such is my love.

~ *D.R. Goodman*

PORTRAIT, BUST

I layer clay and hope he'll coalesce,
begin to plane his jaw and hone his cheek,
his heavy brow, his nose's prow. Distress.
His ear is wrong, I slice it off. I see
a flaw, pry out his eye, the whole not right.
Relief to stroke his cheek or flatten down
odd locks of hair, but still not him. Too slight,
and mean. It seems he now returns my frown.
A man, and yet not mine, this portrait bust.
He stares out coolly from Swiss mountain mud.
I see just why it's failed, and fail it must,
this blend of burial earth and stony blood.
I love the living head, the breathing face.
I fear the sculpture that would take his place.

~ *Susan de Sola*

For the Moment

Any claim that you will live forever
Because I write a poem about our love
Would be absurd. My verse is not that clever.
But in this mortal substance we're made of
I find enough of immortality
To last a lifetime. My words can't bestow
On you the gift your body gives to me
Each moment your embrace lets me let go
Of everything that makes the moment less
Than infinite, and, letting go, lay hold
Of that landscape of everlastingness
Your touch makes palpable as you unfold
What flesh and soul conspire to allow—
We live forever now, and now, and now.

~ Chris O'Carroll

Travel Plans

The pepper tree spilled round us from its source,
and took a lumpish this-way, that-way course,
while dangling hopeful sprays of cinnabar.
You couldn't rest against the grizzled trunk;
its bulby hump, its knurled and craggy scar,
forced you to lean your weight on me instead.
The two of us were just a little drunk,
and sipped the sun-warmed wine to make us bold.

"I'd like to go to Mexico," you said,
"with you, someday, before we're too damn old,"
while in the sky an airplane's vapor trail
politely licked its seal across the sun.
We watched the growing, tantalizing tail,
until it matter-of-factly came undone.

~ *Leslie Monsour*

FOX TROT

How fast the dance, how quick each steps in time
That youth supplies, their feet no stumbling knot,
One, two, one . . . two swing robust in their prime
Toward tango, music's beat securely caught.
The partners change, their movements sing release,
Momentum thrusts their twisting hips to life.
Hands open, clutching, pulsing love's increase.
Then dosie-doe, that dancers' settled wife.
Heart beats the phrase that slowing legs must match.
Three, four, counts fall through tempo's gaping faults.
Their clumsy jig adjusts. A new dispatch.
Arms frame soft movement, quite content to waltz.
The couple's eyes embrace, their souls undressed,
Costumed in sheets, by youth's old dance possessed.

~ Cheryl Carty

The Way It Ended

So time went by and they were middle-aged,
which seemed a crazy joke that time had played
on two young lovers. They were newly caged
canary birds—amused, yet not afraid.
A golden anniversary came around
where roasts were made and laughing stories told.
The lovers joined the laugh, although they found
the joke, but not themselves, was growing old.
She started losing and forgetting things.
Where had she left her book, put down her comb?
Her thoughts were like balloons with broken strings.
Daily he visited the nursing home
to make her smile and keep her in their game.
Death came at last. But old age never came.

~ *Gail White*

LOVE NOTE

Unseen, she tucked it in her lover's coat
while he was busy packing up his clothes
and laptop for a week away. The note
might be discovered on the plane. Who knows?
Or still much later in a hotel room
before he settles into bed alone.
Alone. She feels a sudden sense of doom
about things left undone and things unknown.

What if the letter falls out like a glove
 lost in a crowded airport ticket line,
then stamped by ruthless heels that can't feel love?
She wishes she had sent a clearer sign—
concealed her words where only he could see,
tattooed beneath his skin, indelibly.

~ Kyle Potvin

FEMME FATALE

I must applaud the snake for making truth
Creative right up front, his function more
Than realized, slick character more sleuth
Than devil, dredging knowledge from the core:
Symbolic bark, leaves, fruiting apple's juice
Down Adam's chin. But Eve's the one to watch.
Will Eden's complicated rogue seduce
Her lust for consciousness? Curled in the crotch
Where two limbs split, his hiss becomes embroiled
With words, he falls for her, their acts bring pain
That smites Creation's root, life comes uncoiled—
A denouement with no cathartic strain,
But for sheer pathos I would give this play,
This tragic noir, a thumbs-up anyway.

~ Beth Houston

WOMAN INTO TREE

Greek myth records the known (but hated) fact
that women do not always want men's love.
Some, in the struggle to avoid the act
and keep their would-be mates at one remove,
have called on heaven to destroy their shape.
Most were not answered. Many were betrayed.
But lucky Daphne spoiled Apollo's rape:
her lips grew rough, bark-covered as they prayed;
her raised arms stiffened into boughs to sift
white blossoms on the god's defeated pride.
How many girls inherited the gift
of Daphne? Under flowering lips they hide
the bitter taste of bark, and no one sees
how many sweet words fall from walking trees.

~ *Gail White*

NIKE OF SAMOTHRACE

aka "Winged Victory of Samothrace"
marble sculpture, c. 190 BCE

Alighting on some warship's prow, her wings
Swept back, commanding waves and wind, her strength
Proclaimed in marble mass, where drapery clings
Suggesting motion, action, down the length
Of thighs and powerful legs, airy wisp
Of cloud across her stomach, and the cord
Beneath her breasts binding wings to slight twist
Of waist, express what graceful spirit soared . . .
Her head now gone, or rather lost in light
Above long sculptured shadows, she lifts wise
Immortal wings, no reason but delight,
Pure eros gazing with abandoned eyes . . .
Victors' goddess, ravished, ecstatic, flies
From slacking sails, possessed by her own flight.

~ *Beth Houston*

PENELOPE

There was a woman once who caused a war
From which a single man survived and came
Back to his native land—but not before
His travels added to his soldier's fame.
Circe, the Sirens, and Calypso's isle,
A monster and a princess, played their part
In unforgotten tales. And all the while
Another woman locked him in her heart.
That man was you, my husband. Over sea
And island you adventured. I stayed here,
Keeping the house and weaving endlessly,
And while you followed your immense career,
Blithe as a flying bird, free as a fish,
I lived without a lover. Don't you wish.

~ *Gail White*

THREE GODDESSES

marble sculpture, Phidias, c. 448-432 BCE
The Parthenon and everything in it were made without straight
lines or right angles but were situated to create optical illusions
of straight lines.

A "box" of columns, capitals, curls, curves,

The Parthenon, Athena's temple, holds

Her gold and ivory statue's subtle swerves

That echo in the playful swirling folds

Of drapery roughly shaping bodies smooth

And sensuous: Three Goddesses repose,

Relax in fluid union, ease and move

Themselves, but grant us an eternal pose.

High on their pediment they lean and *s l o w*

-l y laugh their heads off. Stone-thin clothes reveal

Athena balance the immortal flow

Of Artemis and Nike but conceal

    Their touch, in art's museum still displayed

    Through flirting, teasing play of light and shade.

~ Beth Houston

ARIADNE AND THE MINOTAUR

The bull who was and yet was not her brother,
forsaken in the clever walls of Crete—
a creature lost, its nature wholly other.
Not hard to guess the truth that lies beneath
the myth: the fading mention of the child,
the accusations of unnatural birth,
the king who would not have descent defiled;
a child deformed, his life of little worth.
What Ariadne knew: her mother's shame,
the monstrous creature's murderous repute,
its lack of any human given name—
for this she gave her Theseus some jute
that he might go to murder in the maze
and safe, return to hear her sing his praise.

~Lisa Barnett

Theseus

The king gave me protection, and the god
The body of an ad for underwear,
But on the docks of Troezen in a fraud
Of both I tempted every sailor there.

A gray-haired captain who had bowed before
My father's throne now cruised me through the fog
About the ships. I watched him jump to shore,
All muscles, then I led him like a dog.

Winter winds slapped the lines against the mast
He pinned me to. He slipped a tiny head
Into my hand—a horse head sea charm cast
In bronze—to save me from myself, he said.

I murdered all my way to Athens, grim
As Neptune, just to shake the smell of him.

~ *Eric Meub*

JUST RAIN

(for Maz)

You died two months ago, a coastal-town
Recluse. This bloody rain's now making sense.
For you were married to the present tense
And what it brought. In daily life you'd frown
On wilful arrogance. You put it down
To carelessness—a cardinal offence,
You thought—and so you started to dispense
Poetic justice. Margaret, here's your crown.

You celebrated *life*, ignored taboo,
Implored the world at large to do so too,
Adored wild animals, abhorred the zoo,
Championed natural habitats for all,
And didn't give a toss the cuckoo's call
Contained no message.
                So, let the rain fall.

~ *Duncan Gillies MacLaurin*

THE SOLITARY WOMAN

In a pale pink shotgun house in Marigny,
Miz Hillman lived alone. Nobody came
to see her and she had no family,
so, week by week her life was much the same:
she went to church and said the rosary,
took in the mail for neighbors out of town,
adopted cats, watched MSNBC,
and at a rolltop desk she wrote things down—
things no one ever saw, although we guessed
a novel, memoirs, poetry, and more.
We spied no papers though we did our best.
And when she died alone, at eighty-four,
with no companion but a big gray cat,
we pitied her. We were such fools as that.

~ *Gail White*

WOMEN'S WORK

Twelve dollars took the box of antique lace
and linens as the hasty gavel fell.
Later at home unpacking, she can tell
she got a bargain: finely crocheted place-
mats, quaint embroidered guest towels, napkins, heaps
of doilies, table runners—all hand-done.
A woman's work of hours contrived each one
only to wrap and pack away for keeps.
The auctioneer had sketched a few brief clues:
a country homestead, maybe a trousseau
left in a trunk a century ago.
And after all, they're much too good to use.
She smooths away the wrinkles, lays the best
on top, and stores them in her cedar chest.

~ Wendy Sloan

Don't Talk

The books you mean to write; the PhD
you're going back for in divinity;
ideas for an online magazine;
a trip abroad; one more advanced degree,
this time in medicine; a used RV;
an acre on the river near Seguin—
a dozen novel money-making schemes.

The more you plan out loud the less it seems
you have to do to garner satisfaction,
as though the word were equal to the action.
Once voiced, the goal recedes and something new
claims your attention. Superstitiously
I wait to speak about *faits accomplis*.
Brave words become the things we never do.

~ Carol A. Taylor

WEIGHING IN

I'm naked, watched. My body's not alone.
The mirror feasts on fat these plump hands fed.
Consumed, disgraced, while I claim blame's my own,
Old demons raid the banquet in my head.
Why crave sweet taste? Who cooked up appetite!
Which devil should I blame as waist expands?
Scorn, sad disgust, my heart is stuffed with fright
So caught in evil's greasy greedy hands.
My heavy foot, my own thick thunderous thighs,
Why no control? This hand to baby's mouth—
"My life's a joke! This scale is spreading lies."
Sad tubby's cries spread east, west, north to south.
I can't stop! Chubby demons sour my wins
When even health food feeds quadruple chins.

~ *Cheryl Carty*

SIZE FOUR

to the lady invariably seated on my left at lunch

Yeah, right. A salad. Well I should have known
this place got girls pared down to skin and bone.
Now while I've polished off a full-course meal
you're still content to munch that lemon peel
hung on your water glass. Take some more sips.
No love handles obscure those skinny hips.
They're sharp as salsa! Girl, you've got some edge.
Splurge on another cut cucumber wedge.
Do I indulge too much? I'm half-way through
dessert, you've taken all that time to chew
up one tomato. Hey, give me a break.
Your vanity is just too hard to take.
Still, I find solace thinking of the dread
your man feels when it's time to climb in bed.

~ *Wendy Sloan*

V

All Hallows' Eve

Ten days ago the mums appeared to be
as fresh as daisies. Seven ninety-nine
was all they cost—an opportunity
to bring some autumn cheer to me and mine.

Unsheathed and trimmed, the sturdy stalks stood well
haphazardly arranged, the vase antique,
the water fortified. I could not tell
where gold turned red on blossoms at their peak.

Such beauty does not last, of course. Decline
occurs. Now, outer petals droop, most leaves
are curled, the once-clear glass of etched design
displays the dirtiness decay achieves.

So cycles go. Nature will have its way.
Tomorrow I may toss the whole bouquet.

~ *Jane Blanchard*

OCTOBER, AND THE OWLS

October, and the owls again—the chill
and smoke that filter through the terrace screen
are shadowed by a hint of sound. Between
faint calls, a hollow silence; and to will
the sound again, we lean onto the sill,
hold stiff and stop our breathing, strain to glean
some signal from the night. Outside, a scene
of moonlight, pine and cloud, and down the hill,
faint glimmer through the branches. Now, the far
dark bass vibration, syncopated, deep
as breath across some ancient vintner's glass,
king bottles played as flutes: old Balthazar
and Jeroboam call across the steep
cool night in counterpoint—and fade—and pass.

~ *D.R. Goodman*

Iron Gate

Cold rain gusts through October, beats the shed,
    Pulls red, gold, auburn leaves from slippery limbs,
        Rakes sodden browns to compost piles, sunk bed
    Of wilted vegetables, slops leaf mold brims
Of wheelbarrow and birdbath, muddy path
    To muddy puddles, snatches scarecrow's hat
        But leaves his straw head perched on arms of lath,
    Grim afterthought, not even gate squeaks scat
Slick crows that peck at wilted vines and corn
    Stalks shredding, scattering. And when sky slumps
        Her shoulders, kneeling now too grave to mourn
    Her newly buried lover, plump hands clump
        Fall's leafless roses in a thorn bouquet
To pierce each heart that passes through this way.

~ Beth Houston

AUTUMN WISH

I wish for seaside weightlessness once more
before I huddle in a heavy coat
and hide my hands in mittens, and before
I wind a woolen scarf around my throat.
I want the salt and sand to stick to me
as if I were a barnacle or bird,
as light as air and thriving thoughtlessly,
anxieties erased and debts deferred.
Unshod, unscheduled, and uninsulated,
I'd drop my shoulders and I'd lift my head,
my step as careless and uncalculated
as winds and waves by wanton currents led.
I want to walk this beach in weightless ease—
a summer girl once more before the freeze.

~ *Jean L. Kreiling*

THE AUTUMN THIEF

Two days till Halloween, yet with a howl
a snowstorm snuffs the jack o' lantern's eyes.
Does Autumn laugh beneath her lacy cowl,
or does true Winter knock without disguise?
No drugstore-bought confections can bewitch
as richly as this master confiseur.
She glitters cobwebs with her sugar-stitch
and truffles branches like a saboteur
until—*lights out*—they snap like pretzel sticks.
She silvers nightshade berries like dragées,
her mischief sweet, no telling treats from tricks.
Across the hush of stiff meringue, the glaze
of moonlight shines. And so, we hail the thief
whose icing thickly frosts each flame-licked leaf.

~ *Nicole Caruso Garcia*

ICE

As traffic hushes, rain slows, chilled dusk stills.
Fogged windows darken, thinning chimney smoke
Drifts up and hovers, frosted streetlight spills
On hardened puddles. Wrapped in silken cloak,
Ice slips black gloves from sleek black hands that peel
The moon to make sleep potions of eclipse
And spells that freeze park fountains, hands that steal
The verve and verdant stunned by smooth, cold lips
That sip the rain, that tease each pose to change
Into a poise devoid of change, that trick
Each drip to slowly cease to drip: This strange
New liquid, icicle, extends with slick
    Fresh form first form, each solid water slice
    Of light more crystal once it melts to ice.

~ *Beth Houston*

Two Forces Rule the Universe Of Breath

Two forces rule the universe of breath
And one is gravity and one is light.
And does their jurisdiction include death?
Does nothingness exist in its own right?
It's hard to say, lying awake at night,
Full of an inner weight, a glaring dread,
And feeling that Simone Weil must be right.
Two forces rule the universe, she said,
And they are light and gravity. And dead,
She knows, as you and I do not, if death
Is also ruled or if it rules instead,
And if it matters, after your last breath.
But she said truth was on the side of death
And thought God's grace filled emptiness, like breath.

~ Mark Jarman

LEFT OUT

It starts that Wednesday when believers bear
their faith in forehead smudges, and my brow
is pagan-pale. And then they all compare
what they'll give up for forty days, and how
they'll binge on those things later. When they claim
to know that their redeemer lives, I sigh
with envy, even feel a twinge of shame,
because I just don't get it. If I lie—
partake of Alleluias and baked ham
as if they mean what they're supposed to mean—
then they don't taste the way they should; the sham
leaves ashes on my tongue. I haven't seen
the light, I don't believe he did ascend
to heaven—but I wish I could pretend.

~ *Jean L. Kreiling*

A Fine Address To Death

"Death, be not proud": A fine address to Death,
That sadist skeleton, that mocking skull,
That zero sum game threatening to annul
Identity and being with our breath.
Yes, we can gird our courage to defy
That Knight of Nothingness, that Bully Power,
And stand and brave Him in that shining hour
We're given till we really have to die
And go we know not where, though we can guess—
And there's the rub—we're pretty sure we know,
Despite the faith we're eager to profess.
No wonder we're so eager not to go,
Until that time arrives when it seems right
That we go, gentle, into that goodnight.

~ *Bruce Bennett*

Waking on the Northwest Slope

There is no sunrise, this side of the hill—
only a sky on rheostat, whose light
increases to a steely, waking white
with no known source, and leaves untouched the chill

laid down the night before. There is no ray
of warming sunlight bringing up a scene
of bench and garden, flagstone, fountain, green—
to lift me from my torpor into day.

But in the highest eucalyptus crown,
where fog has left its traces, gusty skies
stir up an icy show of scattered light:

a thousand golden suns reflected down
in pinpoint beams; and though I may not rise,
I know the East has seen the end of night.

~ *D.R. Goodman*

CHARLES, FOR HARRIET

I can't help feeling Charles is still alive.
I can't help seeing Charles is simply dead.
"People don't just disappear," Charlotte said.
And what is it that husband is to wife?
—The camaraderies of daily life,
a long, slow warmth and rising heat in bed,
eating together, feeding, being fed,
faith that it will go on, unwatched belief?
Something that interpenetrates the air,
colors every movement, blink of the eye.
They come to look alike while they still try
—dancing apart, and fencing what they share—
to balance unseen and seen in the mirror.
You're too much here. You're much too far. Nowhere.

~ Patrick Daly

MAGGIE

I woke into the sounds of your bad dream,
Reached to your warmth, touched you, and softly said
It's okay, Maggie, I'm here, you're in bed.
Your murmurs slowed, you shifted toward me, seemed

To say my name, then quieted again,
Breathed deep away, my comfort mine to keep.
Not wanting you to lose your thread of sleep,
I kept my kiss, my need to kiss you *then*

But would not call you back from sleep's safe place—
And caught the panic of Eurydice—
That you would go before I let you see
The dying of my heart to touch your face.

You slept away. I knew forever I
Would learn how far off death is when you die.

~ *Mike Carson*

A VISIT ON ALL SAINTS DAY

Hello. I've brought your favorite flowers again.
How is it going under there, my dead?
On this side, we're no better off than when
you walked beside us. (Yes, I know I said
the same last year.) The human race is not
improvable. Ask any saint you meet.
We've gone to war again without a thought.
Our leaders shuffle bribes, our heroes cheat.
Your children haven't turned out awfully well,
but who expected it? You're not to blame,
and anyway, I don't believe in hell.
Goodbye for now. I'm always glad I came.
I make no promises about next year,
but one way or another, I'll be here.

~ Gail White

If God Survives Us, Will His Kingdom Come?

If God survives us, will his kingdom come?
But let's row out to sea and ship the oars
And watch the planet drown in meteors.
If God forgives us, surely he will come.
Can we nail up a man and do the same
To a child? Yes. And drive the spikes through tears.
But let's row out to sea and watch the stars.
No matter what we do, they are the same,
Crossing the bleeding sky on shining feet,
Walking on water toward us, and then sinking.
Surely when he grew up, God must have known
What sort of death was waiting for one thinking
That with his coming history was complete.
We'll greet him as the children would have done.

~ *Mark Jarman*

PSALM

Father, deemed dead and buried everywhere
I look, how could your blessed ghost expire?
You're not slain Osiris strewn down some lair,
Pompeii was not your pyramid of fire,
you were not split like atoms into sprays
of radioactive ash. Museums these days
might be the last temples where godly sight
abounds. They've endeavored to dig you out.
I've sifted through these gods and gleaned no light . . .
then left your vespers as nature mired with doubt.
Yet, in my cage of flesh your Spirit thrums on.
O bless that time I'll strike deadlocked repose:
then you who fed lives to the phoenix, summon
leftover lives as resurrection glows.

~ *Alexander Pepple*

Flying Dreams

One might conclude that paramecia and similar
animalcules regularly rub shoulders with immortality.
   —Wislawa Syzmborska.
In the sweat of thy face shalt thou eat bread, until thou
return unto the ground.
   —Genesis 3:19)

Single-celled creatures do not have to die
and are not born. One becomes two, that's all.
So Eve and Adam, bland before their fall
dream in the cradle of eternity:
they've been here always and always will be.
The wind's the breath of God, on which the call
to know, and be known, is a *hsst!* too small
to break the spell of immortality.
But something blazed—it stunned them with its heat
and when they woke their heels were black and blue.
Limping in the desert, they dreamed they flew.
They might have flown, but now they cannot fly.
They taste salt in everything they eat.
They have each other, and they have to die.

~ *Patrick Daly*

CARDS IN THE PARK

The old men passed around scuffed cards with dry,
loose-fingered hands—an easy way to mark
the slow, familiar hours until dark—
and argued play with cartoon rancor or
spoke lazily of other things, re-read
what they'd been dealt, and watched the shifting sky.

A younger man, whose mind sought patterns, I
would see them as I hurried through the park,
my steps at times impeded by the stark
resemblance of their day to that before,
and how both days were like the lives they led,
the wait for dark so bald a wait to die.

The sorrow wouldn't last; I couldn't stay
To touch it. I, too, had my games to play.

~ *Max Gutmann*

BOB JUMPING

in memoriam Bob Evans

Bob told us he had once stood on a ledge
and tried and tried to get himself to leap
—really no leap at all, a mere six feet
if he had not looked down—over the edge,
down and dizzyingly down. An abyss.
No way back or forward, only rock steep
above and falling off into the deep.
Just jump. Just couldn't. So he didn't budge
all day, until the day began to dim—
and then he laughed, and leapt, and was home free.
Years later, now he's gone. Charlotte said he
had met death the way he lived, willingly
took off when it was time. I might still be
hesitating. I want to jump like him.

~ *Patrick Daly*

FLOATING NUN

Some visitors pledge half their salaries to see the nun magically
floating in a temple pool in Kanchanaburi.
  —Exchange Student Journal, Age 16

I always thought this act an easy way
to earn some *baht*: she'd step into a pool,
allow her pristine robes to soak, then sway
back, buoyant from the salt, relaxed and cool.
But then one summer day last year, I slipped
into the hazy shadows of our lake
and stayed near motionless—back long, face tipped
to meet the sun—rocked in a dying wake.
I heard a rushing rhythm in my ears.
It drowned the voices calling out to me.
I was suspended there like brimming tears,
reminded of the Thai nun floating free:
Her mind at rest, far from the tourist show,
lost in this unmoored state, this letting go.

~ *Kyle Potvin*

RETROSPECTIVE

As quickly as a fragile spirit blinks
and fades into the blue fluorescent glow,
the hum of cold machines—as breathing sinks
and ceases under age's ravage—so
too, fade the bitter memories, the sole
persisting images nostalgic, sweet,
and sorely missed. Forgotten is the whole
dark warp of life. Instead, we weave deceit
and joy into a history our hearts
can bear—or, it is woven by those powers
that shield us from ourselves, obscure the parts
that threaten in survival's crucial hours:
the start, the finish—suffering replaced
like pangs of birth, the sting of death erased.

~ *D.R. Goodman*

THE THREE FATES

The Moirai, the sisters who determine all destinies by spinning wool, are named Clotho, Lachesis, and Atropos. Atropos means "The Unturning."

Clotho takes the raw wool in her hands
And twists it tightly, as if it were bled
From her own heart. She licks it, and the strands
Of oily wool cohere into a thread.

Lachesis winds the spool, and it is said
She gives just what she fancies, nothing more.
You may get ninety years before the tread
Of heartbeat stops, or maybe half a score.

The spool goes to Unturning, and the lore
Tells of her dreaded shears. She snips the run
Of yarn, and then it's over—no encore.
Your petty antics and your words are done.

Three Sisters, with their spindle, spool, and shears,
Who weave the fabric of allotted years.

~ *Joseph S. Salemi*

David Gwilym Anthony was born in Ffestiniog, North Wales, and brought up and educated at Hull Grammar School before going on to study history at St. Catherine's College, Oxford. His poems have appeared in magazines and anthologies in the UK, the USA, Japan, and online. His poetry book is *Passing through the Woods (2012)*. His life has been spent in the near aura of famous poets: Dafydd ap Gwilym, greatest of the Welsh bards; Philip Larkin, one-time librarian of Hull University; and Andrew Marvell, a fellow alumnus of Hull Grammar School. He lives with his wife in Stoke Poges, Buckinghamshire, a stone's throw from the churchyard where Thomas Gray is buried. He is hoping that one day something of these poets will rub off on him.

Lisa Barnett's poems have appeared in *The Hudson Review, Measure, The Orchards, Poetry, Snakeskin, Valparaiso Poetry Review,* the anthology *Sonnets: 150 Contemporary Sonnets,* and elsewhere. She is a three-time Howard Nemerov Sonnet Award finalist and is the author of the chapbook *Love Recidivus.* She lives outside Philadelphia with her husband.

Bruce Bennett is the author of ten collections of poetry and more than thirty poetry chapbooks. His most recent book is *Just Another Day in Just Our Town: Poems New And Selected, 2000-2016* (Orchises Press). His first New And Selected, *Navigating The Distances,* was chosen by Booklist as "One Of The Top Ten Poetry Books Of 1999." He was a co-founder and served as an editor of the literary journals *Field* and *Ploughshares,* and has reviewed poetry in *The New York Times Book Review, The Nation,* and elsewhere. From 1973 until his retirement in 2014, he taught Literature and Creative Writing and directed the Visiting Writers Series at Wells College, and is now emeritus professor of English. In 2012 he was awarded a Pushcart Prize.

Jerome Betts lives in Devon, England, and edits the verse quarterly *Lighten Up OnLine.* His work has appeared in a wide variety of British magazines as well as UK, European, and North American web publications such as *Amsterdam Quarterly, Angle, Autumn Sky Poetry Daily, Better Than Starbucks, The Hypertexts, Light, The Rotary Dial* and *Snakeskin.*

A native Virginian, **Jane Blanchard** divides her time between Augusta and Saint Simon's Island, Georgia. She has earned degrees in English from Wake Forest (B.A.) and Rutgers (M.A., Ph.D.) Universities. Her poetry has been published around the world as well as posted online. Her fourth collection is *In or Out of Season* (2020).

John J. Brugaletta has published eight volumes of his poems, most recently *One of the Loves Was Yours* (2020). He is professor emeritus at California State University Fullerton, and now lives on the redwood coast of California.

Mike Carson lives in Bloomington, Indiana, and is emeritus professor and department chair at the University of Evansville, where he taught medieval and Renaissance English and literature, specializing in Shakespeare and Milton. His poems have appeared in many journals, including *The Southern Review*, *Gulf Stream*, *Measure*, *Five Points*, *New Virginia Review*, and *The Hopkins Review*. His poetry book is *The Keeper's Voice* (Louisiana State University Press)

Jared Carter has published seven poetry collections, including most recently *The Land Itself* and *His Darkened Rooms of Summer: New and Selected Poems*. He has received many literary awards and fellowships, including the Walt Whitman Award; the Poets' Prize; the Pushcart Prize; the Academy of American Poets Prize, Yale University; a Guggenheim Fellowship; a Fellowship from the National Endowment for the Arts; the Indiana Arts Commission Literature Fellowship; and the Margaret Bridgman Fellowship, Bread Loaf Writers' Conference. He lives in Indiana.

Cheryl Carty is a founding board member and dance teacher at Manatee (County) School for the Arts in Florida. She performed nationally and internationally with the American Chamber Ballet Company of Carnegie Hall and for ten years with the Rockettes. She has performed in, choreographed, and directed dozens of shows Off-Broadway and elsewhere, including TV commercials, and has won numerous awards. Later in life she got a BA in Creative Writing at Eckerd College in Florida.

Ted Charnley's work has appeared in journals such as *Passager*, *The Road Not Taken*, *Think*, *The Lyric*, and *The Orchards Poetry Journal*. He lives with his wife in a 200-year-old farmhouse they restored in central Maryland. There, he herds woodchucks, practices chainsaw topiary, and leaves offerings for the nymphs of the springs.

Patrick Daly works for a software start-up and writes poetry on his lunch hours. His poem *Words* was a poem of the year in the *New Statesman*. His poetry has appeared in journals such as *Ekphrasis* and *The Sand Hill Review*, and in the anthologies *The Place that Inhabits Us; A Bird Black as the Sun; Transfer 100;* and *America, We Call Your Name*. His poem *Tiananmen Square* received honorable mention in the Pushcart Prizes, and his chapbook *Playing with Fire* won the Abby Niebauer Memorial Prize. He has published articles and reviews in the *London Times*, the *San Jose Mercury News*, and the *Palo Alto Weekly*. A portion of his poem *The War* appeared in the *New York Times*. He and his wife Charlotte were the founders of *Out of Our Minds*, a prime-time poetry show on KKUP radio in Cupertino, California.

Diane Elayne Dees's poems have been published in many journals and anthologies. She is the author of the chapbooks *Coronary Truth* and *I Can't Recall Exactly When I Died*. Diane lives in Covington, Louisiana, and publishes *Women Who Serve*, which delivers news and commentary on women's international professional tennis.

Susan de Sola is an American poet living in The Netherlands. Her work has appeared in venues such as *The Hudson Review, The Hopkins Review, Birmingham Poetry Review, The Dark Horse,* and *PN Review,* and in anthologies such as *The Doll Collection* and *The Best American Poetry 2018.* She is a winner of the David Reid Poetry Translation Prize and of the Frost Farm Prize for metrical poetry. Her poetry collection is *Frozen Charlotte* (Able Muse Press).

Kevin Durkin attended schools in West Virginia, Pennsylvania, and Germany before earning his degree in English literature from Princeton University. He has taught English in Singapore, Kitakyushu (Japan), New York City, and Washington, D.C. He also has performed in the plays of Shakespeare across the United States. Currently a managing editor at *Light* and at The Huntington Library, Art Museum, and Botanical Gardens in San Marino, California, he resides with his wife and two daughters in Santa Monica.

Nicole Caruso Garcia is Associate Poetry Editor at *Able Muse* and a Board member at Poetry by the Sea: A Global Conference. Her work has been nominated for the Pushcart Prize, Best of the Net, and the Anthony Hecht Poetry Prize, with poems appearing in *Crab Orchard Review, DIAGRAM, Light, Measure, Mezzo Cammin, PANK, Plume, The Raintown Review, Rattle, RHINO, Sonora Review, Spillway, Tupelo Quarterly,* and elsewhere.

Claudia Gary teaches workshops through The Writer's Center in Bethesda, MD. She is a three-time finalist for the Howard Nemerov Sonnet Award and a semifinalist for the Anthony Hecht award. She is the author of *Humor Me* and her chapbooks include *Genetic Revisionism* and *Bikini Buyer's Remorse.* Her poems appear in journals internationally and in anthologies such as *Villanelles; Forgetting Home; The Great American Wise-Ass Poetry Anthology;* and *Love Affairs at the Villa Nelle.* She has chaired panels such as "The Sonnet in 2016," "Poetry and Science," and "Poetry and Music" at poetry conferences at West Chester University and the Robert Frost Farm. Claudia is also a health science writer, visual artist, and composer of art songs and chamber music.

Mel Goldberg taught literature and writing in California, Illinois, Arizona and as a Fulbright Exchange Teacher at Stanground College in Cambridgeshire, England. He took early retirement and moved to Sedona, Arizona, where he completed his first novel and taught literature and writing at Yavapai College. Mel and his wife bought a small motor home and traveled throughout the US, Canada, and Mexico for seven years. His most recent book of haiku is *The Weight of Snowflakes.* His book of poetry is *Memories* (Finishing Line Press). He has also written two detective novels.

Midge Goldberg's sonnets have won and been finalists in the Nemerov Sonnet Award contest four times. Her most recent collection, *Snowman's Code*, was the recipient of the Richard Wilbur Poetry Award. Her poems have appeared in *The Hopkins Review*; *Light*; *Appalachia*; and on Garrison Keillor's *A Writer's Almanac*. She lives in New Hampshire with her family, two cats, and an ever-changing number of chickens.

D.R. Goodman is the author of *Greed: A Confession* (Able Muse Press). Twice winner of the Able Muse Write Prize for poetry, and 2015 winner of the Howard Nemerov Sonnet Award, her work has appeared in journals such as *Crazyhorse*, *Notre Dame Review*, *Seattle Review*, and *Whitefish Review*. Her poems appeared in Ted Kooser's *American Life in Poetry*, and in the anthology *Sonnets: 150 Contemporary Sonnets*. A native of Oak Ridge, Tennessee, she now lives in Oakland, California, where she is founder and chief instructor at a martial arts school.

Benjamin S. Grossberg is Director of Creative Writing at the University of Hartford, in West Hartford, Connecticut. His books include *Space Traveler* and *Sweet Core Orchard*, winner of a Lambda Literary Award and the Tampa Review Prize.

Max Gutmann has contributed to dozens of publications including *New Statesman*, *The Spectator*, and *Cricket*. His plays have appeared throughout the U.S. and have been well-reviewed. His book is *There Was a Young Girl from Verona: A Limerick Cycle Based on the Complete Dramatic Works of Shakespeare*.

Beth Houston has taught creative writing, literature, and composition at ten universities and colleges in California and Florida. Her publications include six poetry books, three nonfiction books, a novel, and over two-hundred poems in dozens of journals such as *Yale Review*, *California Quarterly*, *Massachusetts Review*, *Chicago Review*, *New York Quarterly*, *Blue Unicorn*, and *The Road Not Taken*, as well as anthologies including the *Able Muse Anthology* and *Drive, They Said: Poems About Americans and Their Cars*. *The Literary Review* featured her poetry on Web Del Sol, and in 1999 she was the first featured poet at *Able Muse*.

Mark Jarman is the author of eleven poetry books, most recently *Heronry* (Sarabande Books, 2017). He has published three books of essays and reviews: *The Secret of Poetry*; *Body and Soul: Essays on Poetry*; and most recently, *Dailiness: Essays on Poetry* (2020). With Robert McDowell, he co-authored *The Reaper Essays,* a collection of essays they wrote for their magazine *The Reaper*. He co-edited *Rebel Angels: 25 Poets of the New Formalism* with David Mason. His awards and honors include a Joseph Henry Jackson Literary Award, the Poets' Prize, the Lenore Marshall Poetry Prize, the Balcones Poetry Prize, grants from the National Endowment for the Arts, a Guggenheim Fellowship, and a Chancellor's Research Award from Vanderbilt University. Retired from Vanderbilt, he is Centennial Professor of English, Emeritus.

A.M. Juster has worked in senior positions for four presidents, including a term as Commissioner of Social Security. He is the only three-time winner of the Howard Nemerov Sonnet Award and has also won the Richard Wilbur Award, the Barnstone Translation Prize, and the Alzheimer's Association's Humanitarian of the Year Award. His poems and translations have appeared in *Poetry, The Hudson Review, The Paris Review,* and *Rattle,* and his tenth book is *Wonder and Wrath* (Paul Dry Books).

Jean L. Kreiling is the author of two poetry collections, *Arts & Letters & Love* (2018) and *The Truth in Dissonance* (2014). Her work appears widely in print and online journals; it has been honored with the Able Muse Write Prize, the Great Lakes Commonwealth of Letters Sonnet Award, the Kelsay Books Metrical Poetry Award, a Laureates' Prize in the Maria W. Faust Sonnet Contest, three New England Poetry Club prizes, and the *String Poet* Prize.

Duncan Gillies MacLaurin was born in Glasgow in 1962. He attended boarding schools in Perthshire from the ages of eight to eighteen. He started reading Classics at Oxford University but left without a degree. In 1986, he met the Danish writer Ann Bilde in Italy, and they have been a couple ever since. Settling in Denmark, he took degrees in English and Latin and has taught these subjects at gymnasiet (high-school level) since 1995. His collection of sonnets is *I Sing the Sonnet* (2017).

Peter Meinke was the first Poet Laureate of St. Petersburg, and now is Poet Laureate of Florida. He recently received the Florida Humanities Lifetime Literary Award for Writing. He has published eight collections in the prestigious Pitt Poetry Series, and his book of essays, *To Start With, Feel Fortunate,* received the William Meredith Award. *The Piano Tuner,* a collection of short stories, received the Flannery O'Connor Award. He has won awards from the National Endowment for the Arts, the Poetry Society of America, and the Fulbright organizations, and has given readings throughout America, including at the Shakespeare Library and the Library of Congress. In 2016 he received the SunLit Festival Lifetime Achievement Award for "his outstanding contribution to Letters." He is emeritus professor at Eckerd College and was the Darden Chair in Creative Writing at Old Dominion University. His wife, artist Jeanne Clark Meinke, has illustrated many of his books, including his children's book, *The Elf Poem.*

Eric Meub is the Director of Design for Healthcare at HDR, a global engineering and architecture firm. He is a graduate of the University of California at Berkeley and the Harvard University Graduate School of Design. Eric has won awards for architectural design, including the Paris Prize and the Boston Society of Architects Kelly Prize. His clients include several large health systems and academic medical centers. A native of the San Francisco Bay Area, Eric currently works in Los Angeles and lives in Pasadena. His poetry is often inspired by portraits drawn by his dearest friend Susan.

Born in Hollywood, California, **Leslie Monsour** was raised in Mexico City, Chicago, and Panama. She has been a poetry instructor in Los Angeles public schools and U.C.L.A. Extension, in addition to serving as a mentor for PEN and presenting seminars and master classes at a number of universities and institutions. The author of two poetry collections, Monsour's poems, essays, and translations have appeared in dozens of publications. She is the recipient of a Fellowship in Literature from The National Endowment for the Arts as well as five Pushcart Prize nominations.

Chris O'Carroll is a *Light* magazine featured poet and author of *The Joke's on Me*. His poems also appear in *Love Affairs at the Villa Nelle, New York City Haiku, Poems for a Liminal Age,* and *The Great American Wise Ass Poetry Anthology*.

Alexander Pepple is an electrical and software engineer. His poetry, fiction, and essays have appeared in *Euphony, Snakeskin, Ecclectica, Light, Chronicles, Per Contra, Think, River Styx, Barrow Street, American Arts Quarterly, Measure,* and elsewhere. He founded and edits *Able Muse* and its related presses, and directs its related *Eratosphere* online literary workshop. He edited the *Able Muse Anthology* (2010)

Kyle Potvin's chapbook, *Sound Travels on Water,* won the Jean Pedrick Chapbook Award. She is a two- time finalist for the Howard Nemerov Sonnet Award. Her poems have appeared in *Bellevue Literary Review, Whale Road Review, Tar River Poetry, Ecotone, The New York Times,* and others. Her poetry collection is *Loosen* (Hobblebush Books). Kyle lives in southern New Hampshire.

Katherine Quevedo was born and raised near Portland, Oregon, where she works as an analyst and lives with her husband and two sons. She received honorable mention in the Helen Schaible International Sonnet Contest, and her poetry has appeared in *Songs of Eretz Poetry Review, The Decadent Review, NonBinary Review, Sidequest,* and elsewhere.

Joseph S. Salemi teaches in the Department of Classical Languages at Hunter College, C.U.N.Y. in New York City. He has authored seven books of poetry, including the epic satire *A Gallery of Ethopaths*. His scholarly articles, reviews, and critical essays have appeared in journals world-wide, and he is the editor of the poetry magazine *TRINACRIA*. Essays on the work of famous poets and a selection of his poetry can be seen online at The Society of Classical Poets and at *Expansive Poetry On-Line*. He is married to Helen Palma, a translator of Baudelaire.

Wendy Sloan practiced labor and civil rights law before returning to poetry. Her first collection is *Sunday Mornings at the Caffe Mediterraneum* (Kelsay Books, 2016). Her poems and Italian translations have appeared in journals and in anthologies such as *The Able Muse Translation Anthology Issue, The Best of the Raintown Review, The Great American Wise Ass Poetry Anthology, Love Affairs at the Villa Nelle,* and *Poems* *for a Liminal Age,* benefiting Medecins Sans Frontieres, UK. She has been a finalist in the Howard Nemerov Sonnet Award Competition, and several of her poems have been nominated for a Pushcart Prize. Sloan lives in New York City, where she co-hosts the Carmine Street Metrics poetry reading series.

Elizabeth Spencer Spragins is a poet and writer who taught in community colleges for more than a decade. Her work has been published extensively in Europe, Asia, and North America. She is the author of *The Language of Bones: American Journeys Through Bardic Verse* and *With No Bridle for the Breeze: Ungrounded Verse.*

David Stephenson lives in Detroit, MI and works as an engineer. His poems have most recently appeared in *Blue Unicorn, The Lyric, Snakeskin,* and *The Orchards.* His collection *Rhythm and Blues* (2008) won the Richard Wilbur Award and was published by the University of Evansville Press.

Carol A. Taylor is a poet and retired language teacher living in the greater Houston area. Her work has appeared in various print and online journals and anthologies. She writes almost exclusively in meter, and enjoys playing with form. Much of her verse is light. Carol served as Administrator of *Able Muse*'s Eratosphere from 2001 to 2007.

Tim Taylor lives in Meltham, West Yorkshire, UK. His poems have appeared in anthologies and in various magazines such as *Acumen, Orbis, Pennine Platform,* and *The Lake.* His first poetry collection is *Sea Without a Shore* (Maytree Press, 2019), and he has published two novels.

Gail White is a formalist poet living on Bayou Teche, Louisiana. She is a contributing editor of *Light* and has had work in *Alabama Literary Review, Atlanta Review, Measure,* and other journals, as well as the anthologies *Villanelles; Killer Verse; Love Poems at the Villa Nelle;* and *Nasty Women Poets.* She also co-edited *The Muse Strikes Back* and edited the anthologies *Landscapes With Women* and *Kiss and Part.* Her most recent book, *Asperity Street,* was a special honoree of the 2014 Able Muse Book Award. Her latest chapbook is *Catechism.* She won the Howard Nemerov Sonnet Award in 2012 and 2013 and was the competition judge in 2015. Loves cats.

Debra Wierenga holds an MFA from Bennington College. Her poems have appeared in *The Hudson Review, Poet Lore, The London Review, Measure, The Literary Review,* and other journals. Her chapbook is *Marriage and Other Infidelities.* She lives in Michigan.

Thomas Zimmerman teaches English, directs the Writing Center, and edits *The Big Windows Review* at Washtenaw Community College, in Ann Arbor, Michigan. His latest chapbooks are *Zimmerman on Zimmerman: Sonnets for Bob Dylan* and *Songs We Darkly Know.*

ACKOWLEDGMENTS

Water Bearer, *Avatar Review*; Making It, *Tipton Poetry Journal*; To the Poet Who Thinks I Praise Promiscuously, *The Alarming Beauty of the Sky*; Shakespearean Sonnet, *The Spectator*; At the Summer Poetry Festival, *The House Sitter*; The Poet, Trying to Surprise God, *Liquid Paper*; Slush Pile, *Lighten Up Online*; Tough Professor Sonnet, *Zinc Fingers*; On My Blindness, *The Road Not Taken*; The Movie Screen, *Paper Cinema Anthology*; Wet Day In The Reading Room, *Angle*; On Esperance Bay, *Lucid Rhythms*; Sonnet for Poe, *Verse-Virtual*; Sonnet on the Death of the Man Who Invented Plastic Roses, *Liquid Paper*; Dunderhead, *The Chimaera*; At the Museum of the Book, *Passager*; On Learning the Harvest Moon Is an Optical Illusion, *Snowman's Code*; Starlight, Star Bright, *The Lyric*; Lunar Eclipse, *Measure*; The Sunset Watchers, *The Orchards Poetry Journal*; Meteor Shower, *Iambs & Trochees*; To a Catalpa, *14 by 14*; The Face of Things, *Able Muse*; Harmonics, *The Hudson Review*; Lyrics from a Distance, *The Road Not Taken*; Whale Watch, *Newburyport Anthology*; Lines In Baked Clay, *Amsterdam Quarterly*; Web, *The Dark Horse*; No Help, *Bright Hill Anthology*; The Hoarder, *Measure*; Moose, *Mezzo Cammin*; Over the Edge, *Autumn Sky Poetry Daily*; Hands Folded To Construct a Church and Steeple, *Questions for Ecclesiastes*; In the Alto Section, *The Pennsylvania Review*; Seasonal Song, *Hampden-Sydney Poetry Review*; Winged Presence, *Snakeskin*; Amazing To Believe, *Questions for Ecclesiastes*; The Road Taken, *Susquehanna Quarterly*; Paper Town, *First Things*; One-Way Ticket, *Carnelian*; Roadside Crosses, *The Formalist*; Shades of Venice, *The Shit Creek Review*; Hotel Balcony, *The Alarming Beauty of the Sky*; Los Angeles Fog, *First Things*; On the Death by Drowning of My Favorite New Orleans Restaurant, *Measure*; Sightseers, *Poetry*; Navigator, *Shit Creek Review*; Bryce Canyon, *Umbrella*; Eilean Munde, *Glass: Facets of Poetry*; Bloodlines, *Poetry Scotland*; The Weight, *The Orchards Poetry Journal*; Charm Bracelet, *Blue Unicorn*; To the Hillslope, *Santa Clara Review*; Palm Springs Desert Dystopia, *The Dark Horse*; Tree Fall, *Think Journal*; Habitat, *Angle*; Of Soldiers and Others, *The Formalist*; Anthem, *Measure*; Out of the Night, *Candelabrum*; Moscow Zoo, *The Formalist*; Biting the Hand, *Angle*; Earthbound, *The Healing Muse*; Duck Dignity, *Poetry Porch*; Damaged Goods, *The Orchards Poetry Journal*; To A Mismatched Pair: A Valentine, *The Formalist*; Onset, *Raintown Review*; A Day in June, *American Arts Quarterly*; Fugitive Son, *The Formalist*; Toddler Beneath a

Jacaranda, *Alabama Literary Review*; Recreation, *Tar River Poetry*; Fireball, *The Powow River Poets Anthology II*; Counterfeiter, *Mezzo Cammin*; No Bloody Way!, *The Flea*; Life Drawing, *Measure*; Chess With Monsieur Joffroy, *Chess Magazine*; On Getting a Record Player For Christmas, *Lucid Rhythms*; The Big Smoke, *Snakeskin*; Elegy for a Preschool Teacher, *Elegy for a Preschool Teacher*; Talking to Lord Newborough, *First Things*; Father of the Man, *Worm*; Walking with a Daughter in My Arms, *Lagniappe*; Astrolabe, *Measure*; The End, *Angle*; Three Kings Day, *Raintown Review*; Golden Gloves, *Society of Classical Poets*; The Roaring, *The Orchards Poetry Journal*; Psychomythic Mirror, *Little Rose Magazine*; Again Today, *Angle*; Not Home, *The Orchards Poetry Journal*; Forbidding Fruit, *The Rotary Dial*; The Hard Work of Dying, *The 2019 Hippocrates Prize Anthology*; Cancer Prayer, *Edge City Review*; Anecdotal Evidence, *Measure*; Protocol, *Emrys Journal*; An Absence, *Measure*; On the Suicide of a Friend, *Artemis*; No, *The Formalist*; The Hotel Room, *Orbis*; Sonnet For Her Husband, *Dark Horse*; Love Recidivus, *Poetry*; The Raft, *Poetry Midwest*; Release, *Pulsar*; Sanctuary, *Allegro*; A Girl Like You, *A Girl Like You*; Solace, *Poet Lore*; Phonograph, *Medicinal Purposes*; The Gist Of It, *Slant*; Nobody's Perfect, *Expansive Poetry Online*; Snow White's Plea to the Huntsman, *Mezzo Cammin*; No Love Lost, *Able Muse*; Blackberrying, *Sinister Wisdom*; Lovesick Sonnet #2, *Lovesick Anthology*; Desires are Interchangeable, *The Formalist*; The Gift, *Tiny Flames*; Spouses Who Fight Live Longer, *14 by 14*; Heathcliff, *A Girl Like You*; Mass Mailing Invitation, *Measure*; Regret, *14 by 14*; Our Letters, *Measure*; Love Sonnet, *Seattle Review*; Portrait, Bust, *American Arts Quarterly*; For the Moment, *Iambs & Trochees*; Travel Plans, *Poetry*; The Way It Ended, *Measure*; Love Note, *Measure*; Femme Fatale, *The Road Not Taken*; Woman into Tree, *Measure*; Nike of Samothrace, *Able Muse*; Penelope, *The Lyric*; Three Goddesses, *Able Muse*; Ariadne and the Minotaur, *The Formalist*; Just Rain, *The Barefoot Muse*; The Solitary Woman, *Measure*; Women's Work, *Measure*; Size Four, *Umbrella Journal*; All Hallows' Eve, *Silkworm*; Autumn Wish, *Mezzo Cammin*; The Autumn Thief, *Mezzo Cammin*; Ice, *Able Muse*; Two Forces Rule the Universe Of Breath, *Questions for Ecclesiastes*; A Fine Address To Death, *Innisfree Poetry Journal*; Waking on the Northwest Slope, *Measure*; Maggie, *The Hopkins Review*; A Visit On All Saints Day, *Measure*; If God Survives Us, Will His Kingdom Come?, *Questions for Ecclesiastes*; Psalm, *Measure*; Flying Dreams, *Caesura*; Cards In the Park, *Think Journal*; Floating Nun, *Measure*

Beth Houston, MFA (San Francisco State University), has taught creative writing, literature, and composition at ten universities and colleges in California and Florida, has worked as a writer and editor, and has conducted numerous creative writing workshops. Her publications include books six poetry books, three nonfiction books, a novel, and over two-hundred poems in dozens of journals such as *Yale Review, Feminist Studies, California Quarterly, Massachusetts Review, Chicago Review, New York Quarterly, Blue Unicorn, American Literary Review, South Carolina Review, The Florida Review, 13th Moon,* and *The Road Not Taken,* as well as anthologies including the *Able Muse Anthology* and *Drive, They Said: Poems About Americans and Their Cars. The Literary Review* featured her poetry on Web Del Sol, and she was the first featured poet at *Able Muse.*